HENNING STRASS BURGER

ALPHAKEVIN

KERBER ART

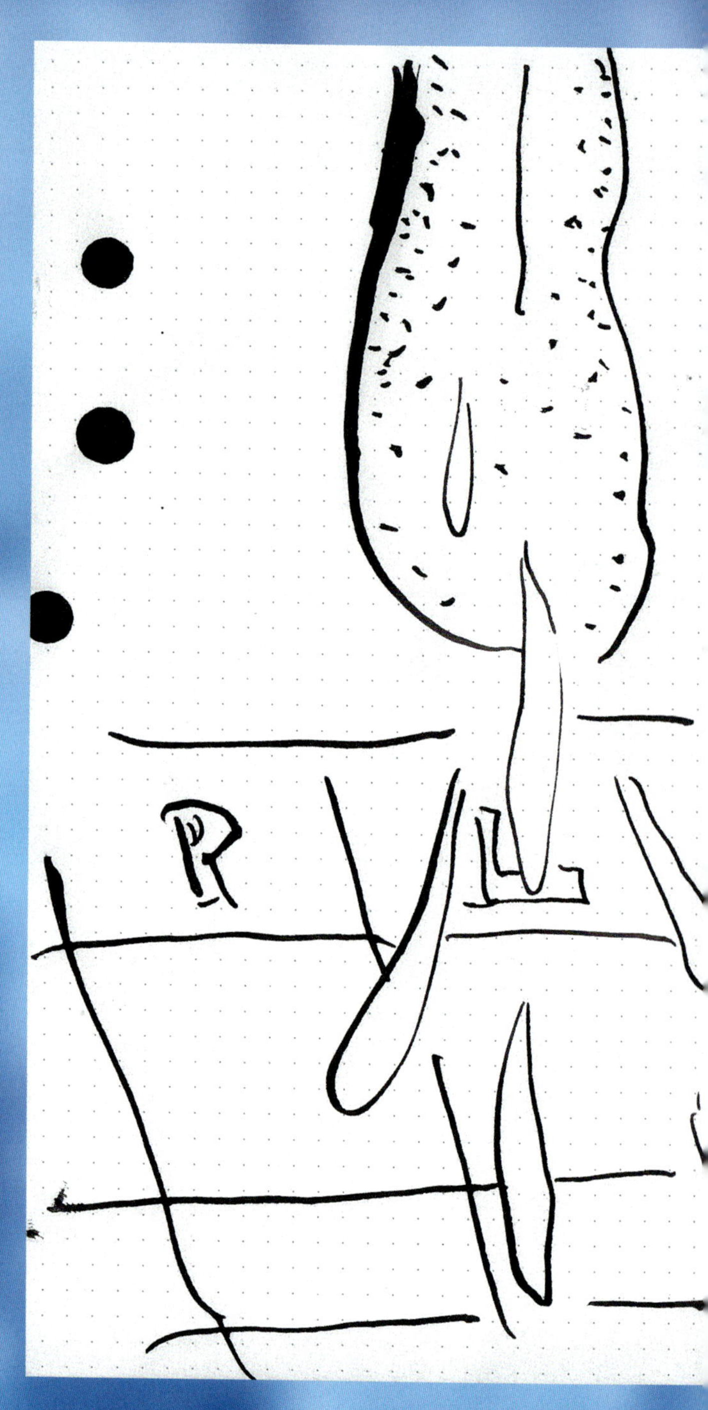

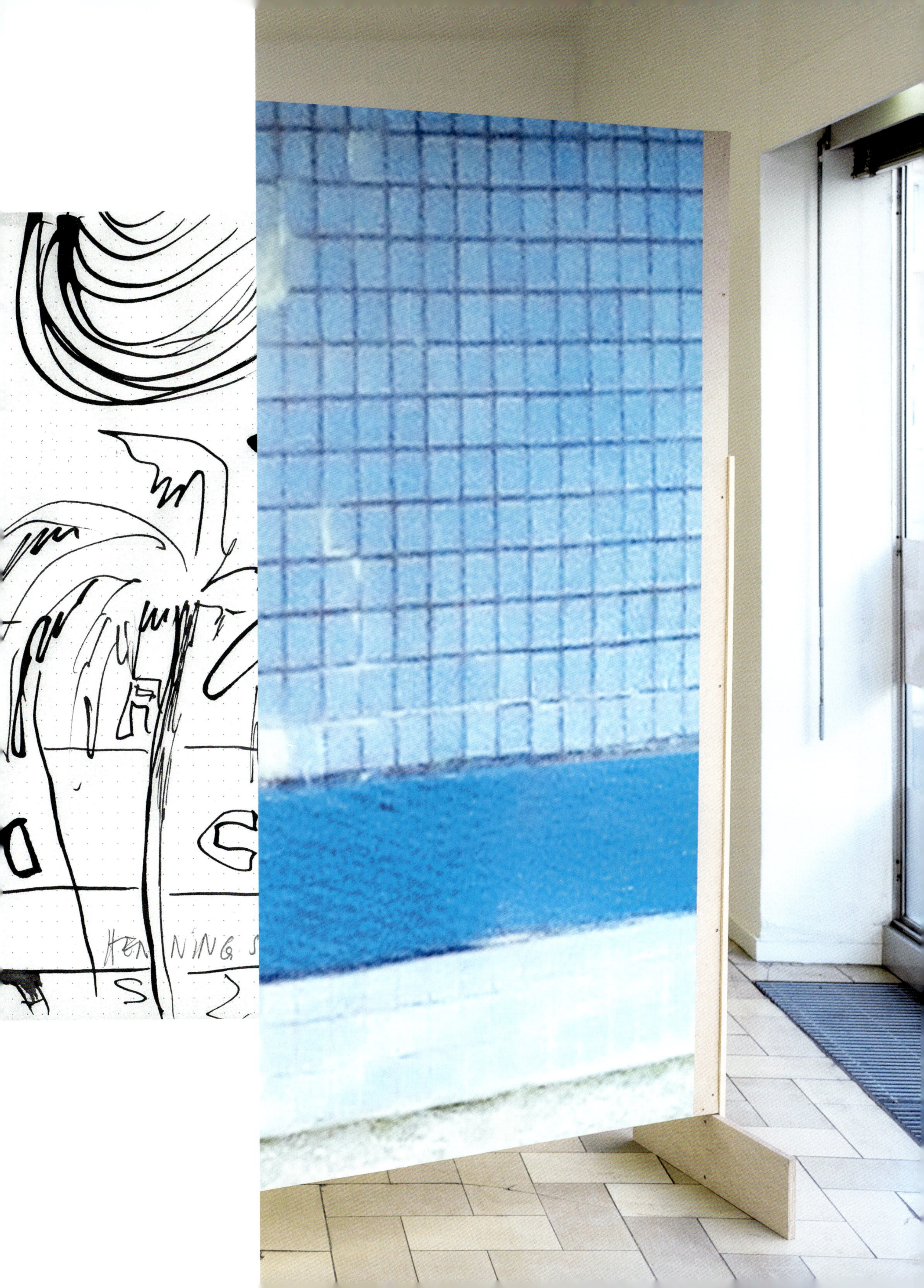
KENNING S

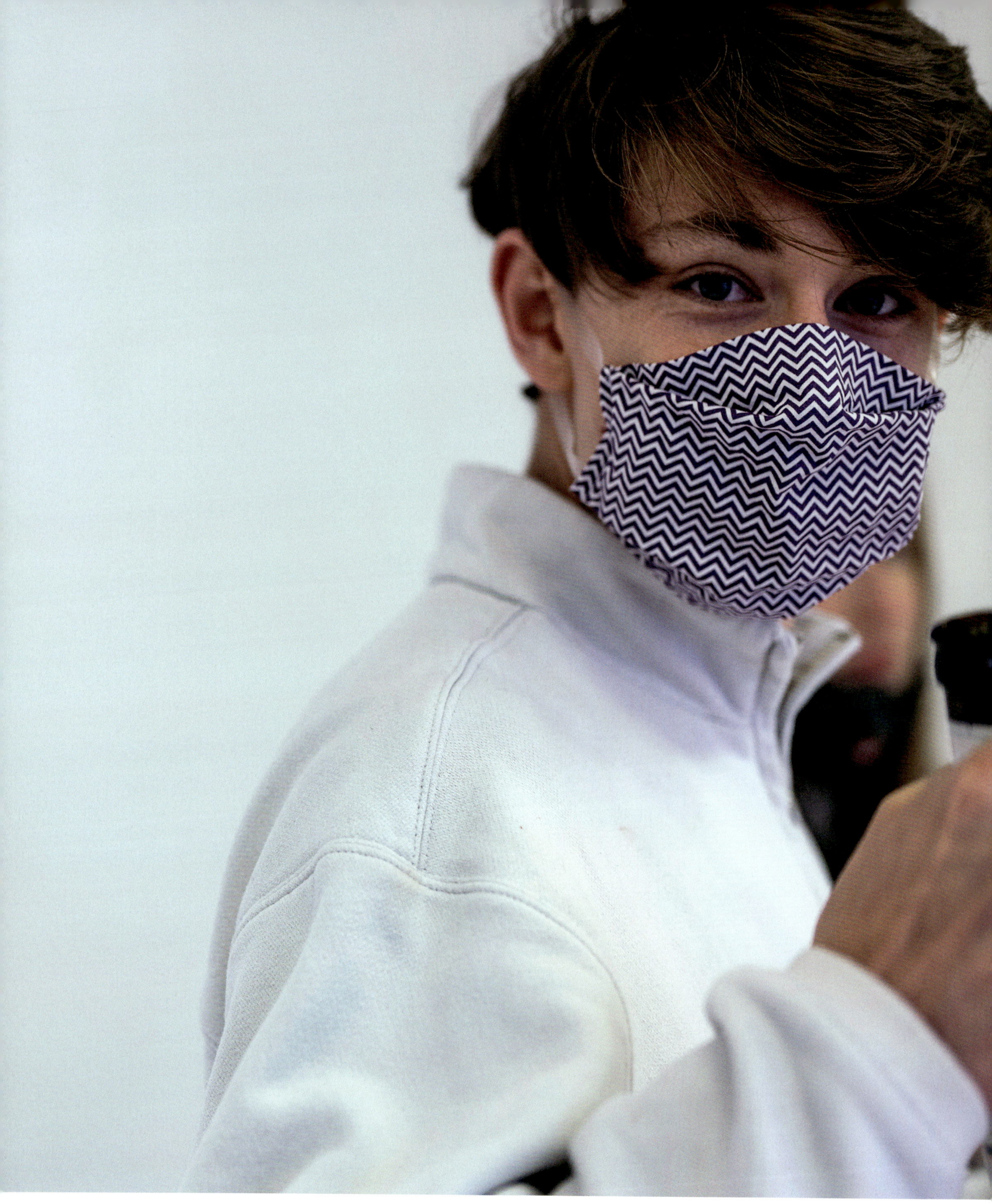

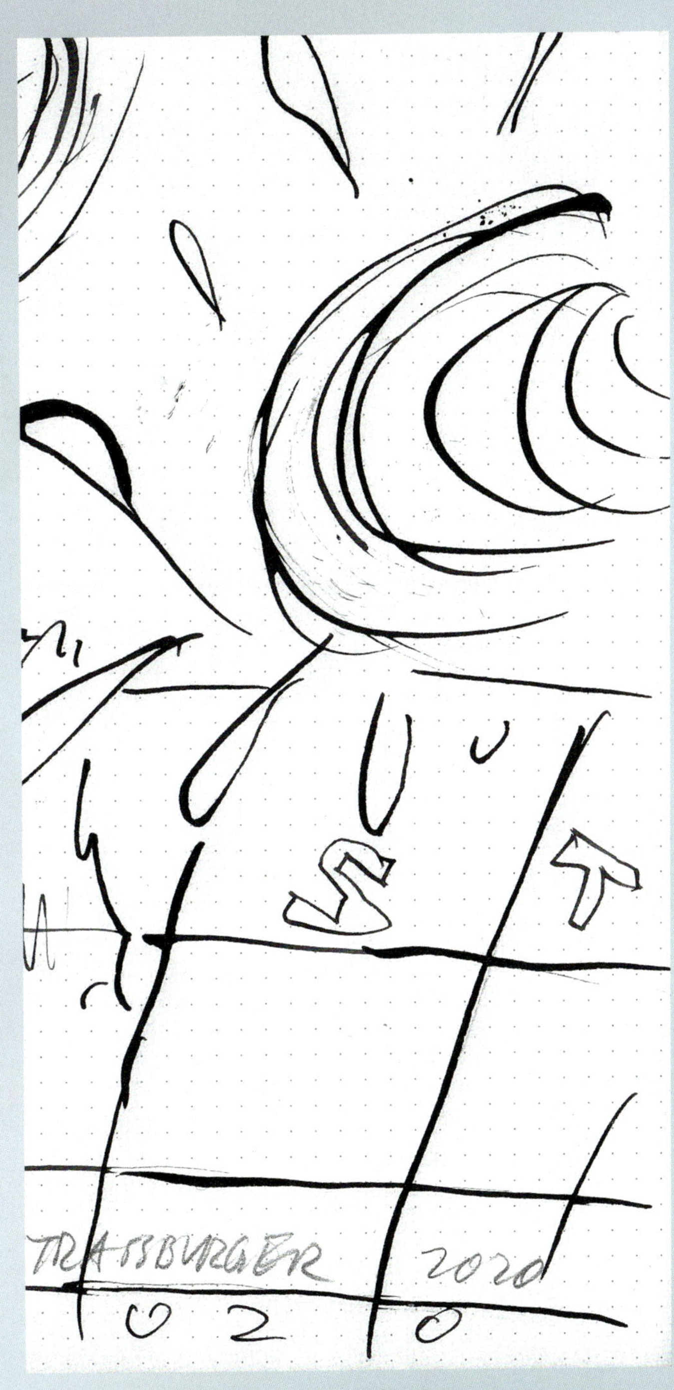
TRASSBURGER   2020

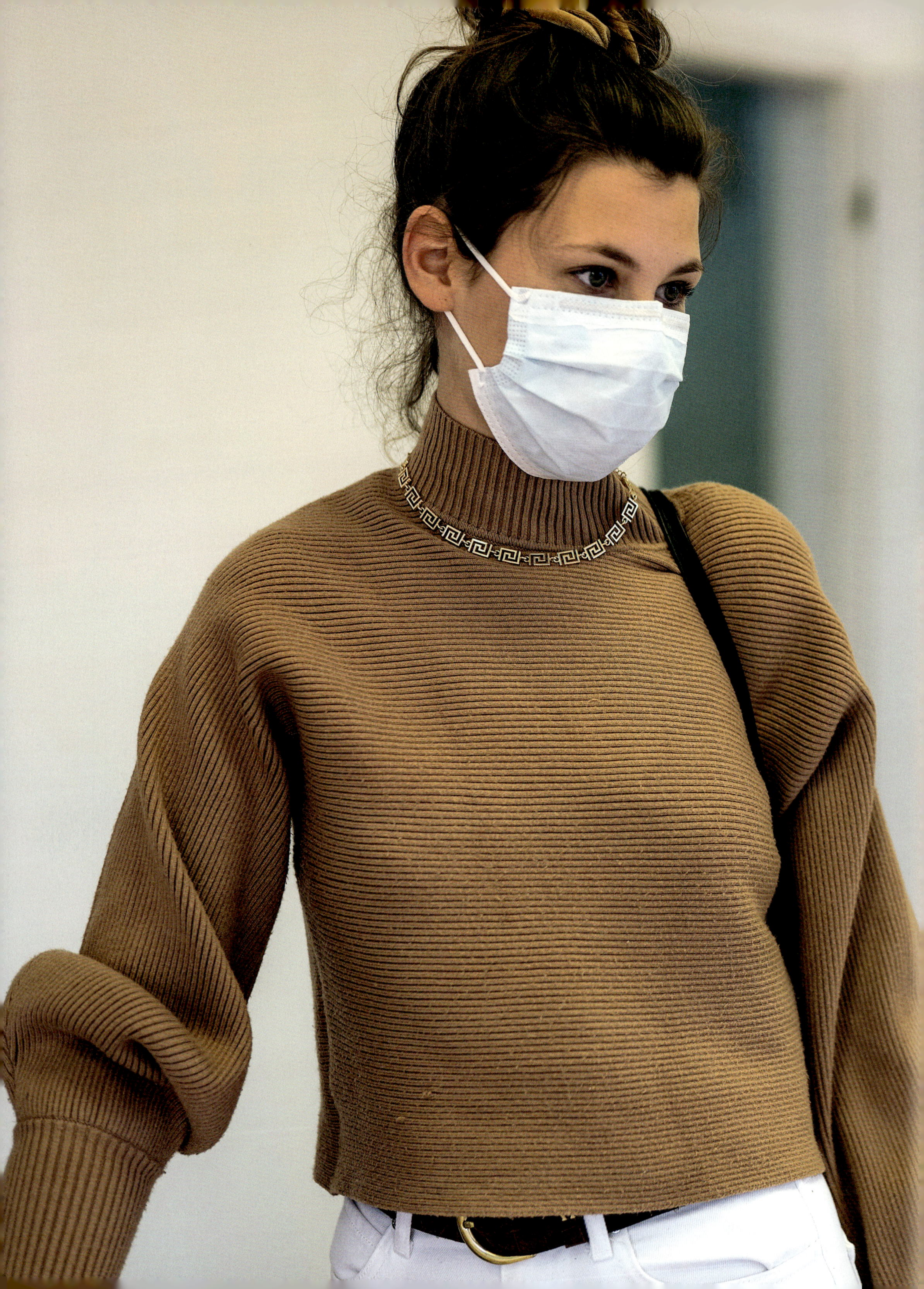

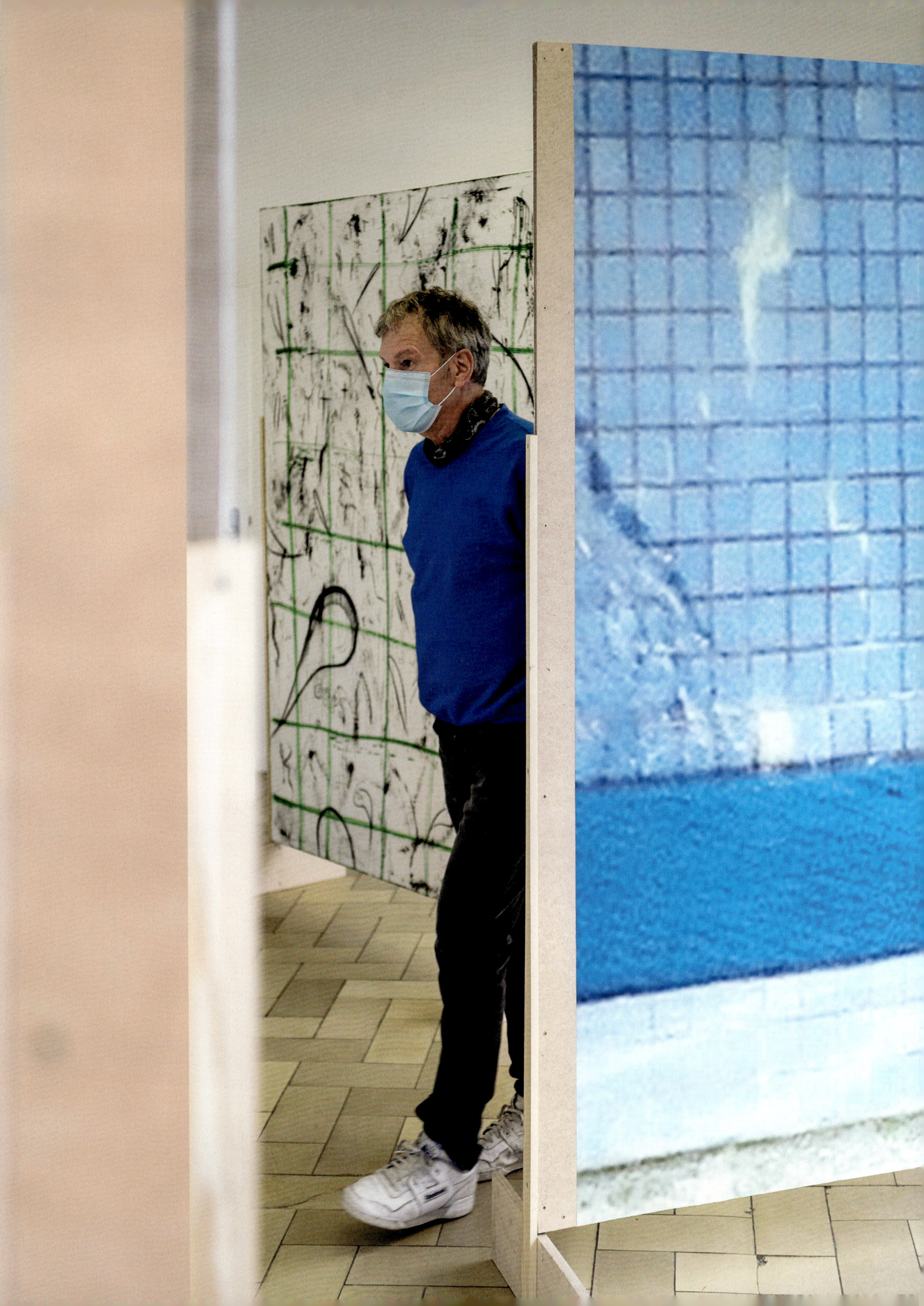

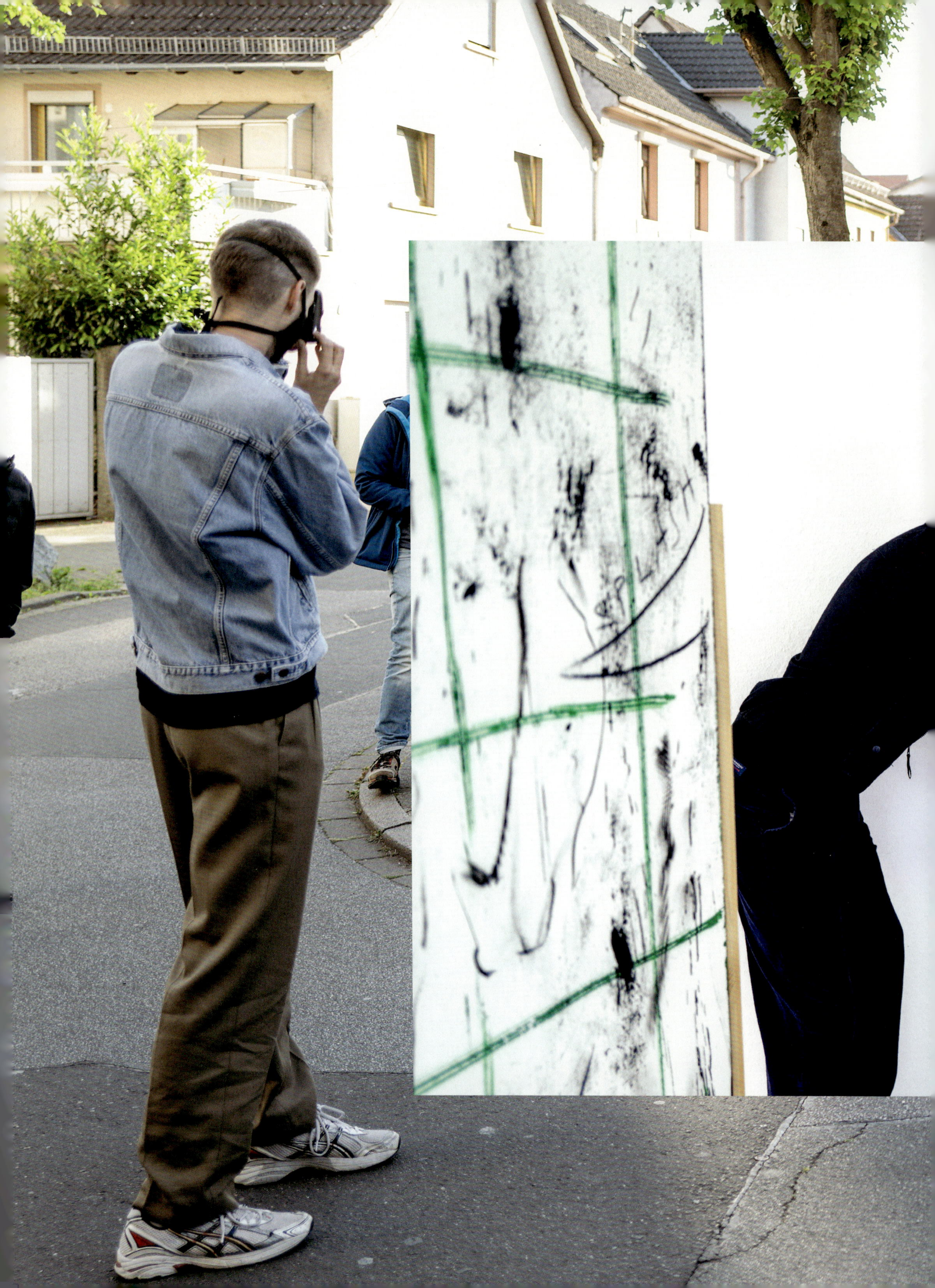
P L A S H

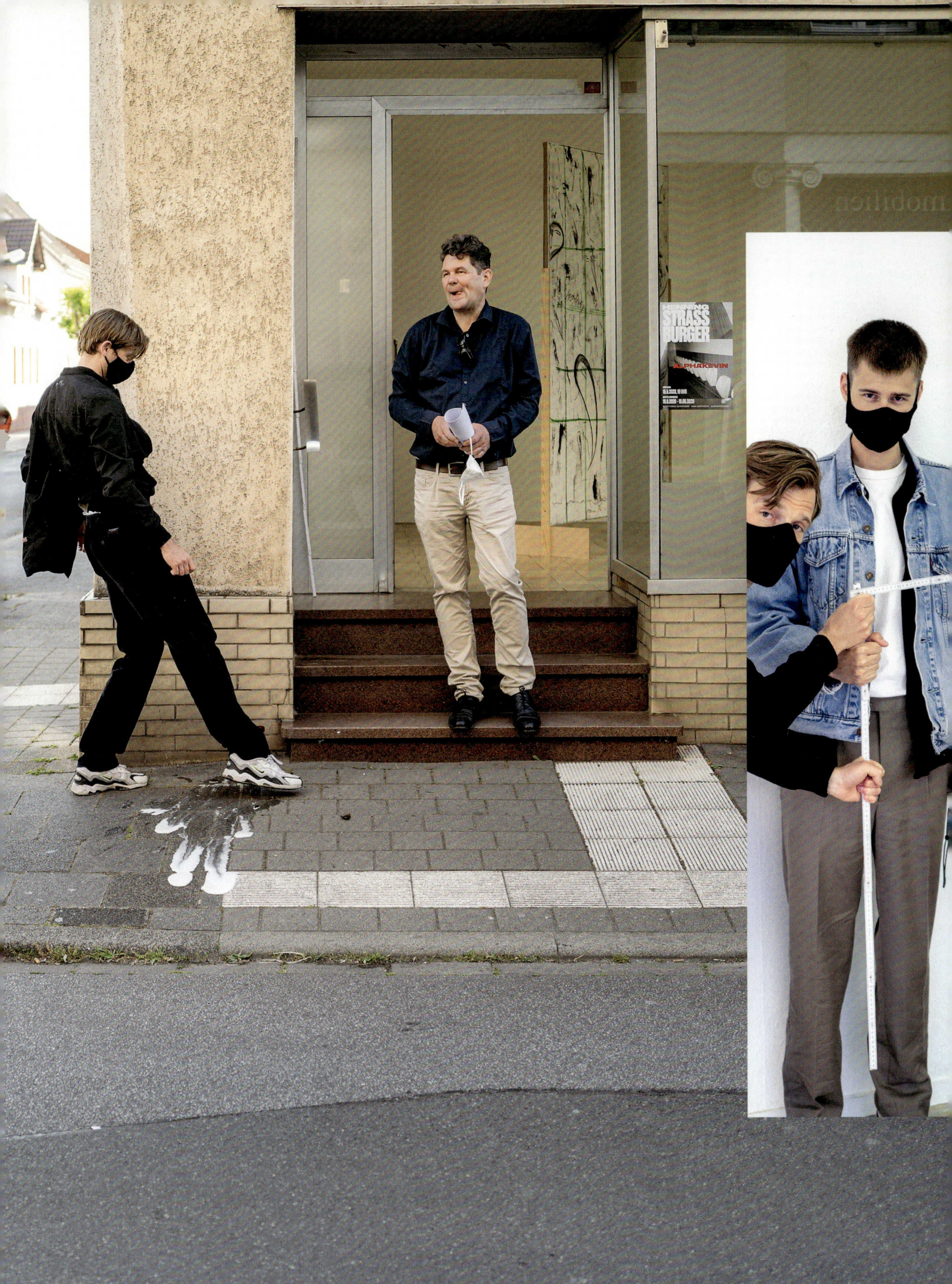
HENNING
STRASS
BURGER
ALPHAKEVIN
15.5.2020, 19 UHR
16.5.2020 – 15.06.2020
mobilien

ANDREAS BREUNIG

HENNING STRASSBURGER

ANDREAS BREUNIG

**Weißt Du, was ich als absolute Qualität am KVHP sehe?
Den absoluten Wahnsinn, der da herrscht. Gute Dynamik.
Du hast ja schon 2011 einen rausgehauen – „Softidrink"! –,
ganz am Anfang. Waren die schon immer so?**

HENNING STRASSBURGER

Damals war das Verrückte, dass ich nicht wusste, was da passiert. Dass eine gewisse Eskalation von den Veranstaltern regelrecht forciert wird. Der Überraschungseffekt war dadurch größer. Klassischerweise wird die Eskalation ja von den Künstlern erwartet. Dort wird das gleich vom Kunstverein aus mitgeliefert. Das ist eher einmalig, würde ich sagen. Vielleicht denkt man sich deshalb auch immer etwas Besonderes aus. Wir haben beide zum Beispiel in Heppenheim Malerei eher installativ präsentiert. Liegt das am Raum oder an uns? Warum können wir nicht einfach die Bilder an die Wand hängen?

Katalog / catalogue **SoftiDrink**, 2011
Kunstverein Heppenheim
Foto / photo: Liv Matthiesen

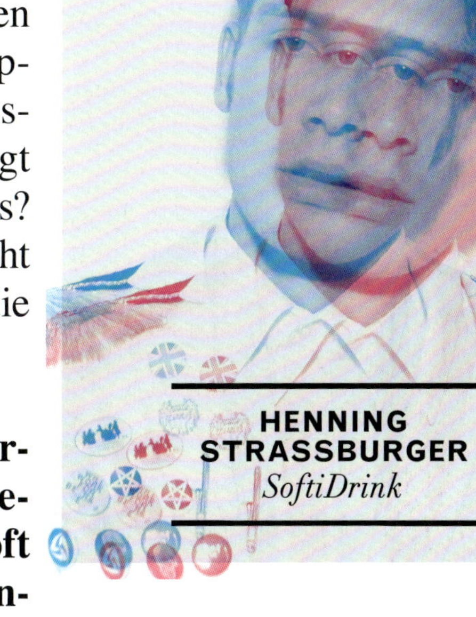

Ich denke, der Raum kommt unseren formalen Präsentationsvorstellungen entgegen. Zumal sich Deine Konzepte doch oft um die Frage drehen, wie Malerei im Kontext zum aktuellen Medienkonsum funktionieren kann. Da braucht's nicht unbedingt 'ne Wand. Oder lieg' ich da falsch? Und außerdem sehen Bilder an der Wand im KVHP scheiße aus.

Das stimmt, die olle Raufasertapete will einfach kein Bild auf sich akzeptieren. Daher hatte ich mir diesmal gedacht, ich mache die Bilder als eine Art Display-Panels mitten im Raum. Mit den Fehldrucken der Hintergrundtapete meiner Ausstellung „Karma Mansion" in London letztes Jahr. Der ursprüngliche Umraum der Malerei wurde dann jetzt in Heppenheim selbst zum malerischen Objekt. Ich fand, das hat ganz gut hingehauen.

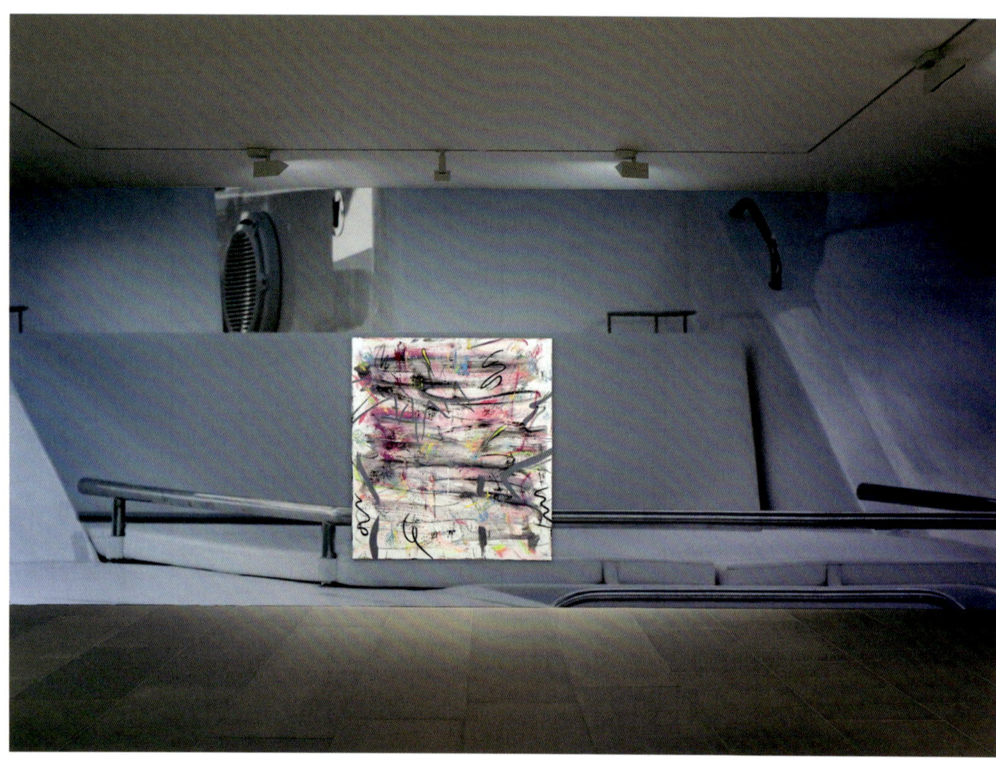

Zusammen mit Jana hast Du ja in Heppenheim extra einen Wettbewerb veranstaltet und die Stadt mit Wahlplakaten zugepflastert und man konnte wählen, wer der Gewinner ist. Da Du der Gewinner warst, konntest Du Deine Ausstellung „Play me / Have no Probs" machen. Woher kommt die Jagd nach dem Thrill, der Gewinner sein zu wollen? Ist Malen = Gewinnen?

KARMA MANSION, 2019
Blain|Southern, London
Foto / photo: Peter Mallet

Naja, den Battle hatten wir gewählt, um Objektivität im Raum zu schaffen. Durch massive Subjektivität im Kontext. Denke, es geht beim Malen eher darum, das Scheitern zu vermeiden. Wenn man dafür gewinnen muss, gut. Aber mal im Ernst, wo ist der Gegner? Den Wettbewerb hat man doch mit sich selbst. Klar fahr' ich nach Heppenheim und sag' mir vorher: „Meine Show muss mehr knallen als die vom Hennich." Aber hinterher waren beide fein. Oder nicht?

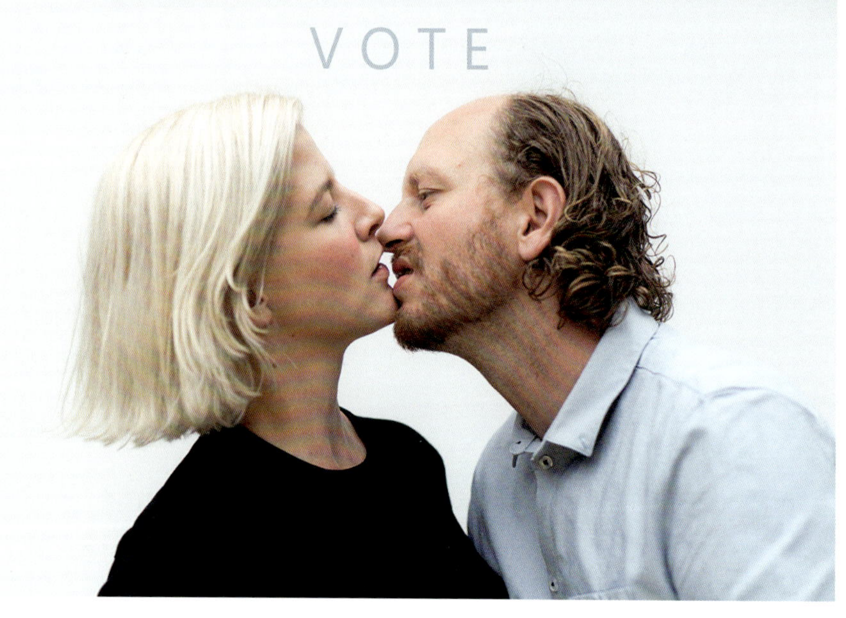

"VOTE Jana Schröder &
Andreas Breunig, 2019"
Kunstverein Heppenheim
Foto / photo: Nicole Schäfer

Total, ich bin ja auch extra nochmal hingefahren, um ein Ründchen Tischtennis in Deiner Installation zu spielen. Da hab' ich das dann auch erst gerafft: Malerei als Werbebanner. Werbung

12

für sich selbst quasi. Aber ich muss auch zugeben, dass ich den
Wettbewerb schon sehe. Deswegen hieß das bei mir vielleicht auch
„ALPHAKEVIN", so als stumpfes Reviergehabe.

**Mir ist dabei übrigens aufgefallen, dass Du in Deinen letzten
Ausstellungen dem Tafelbild (uhh, das Wort ist schlimm) mehr
Raum einräumst. Bei CFA vor allem, top Bilder. Muss man ab
Mitte Dreißig dann doch verstärkt an die Kernproblematik
ran? Die Frage treibt mich zurzeit um.**

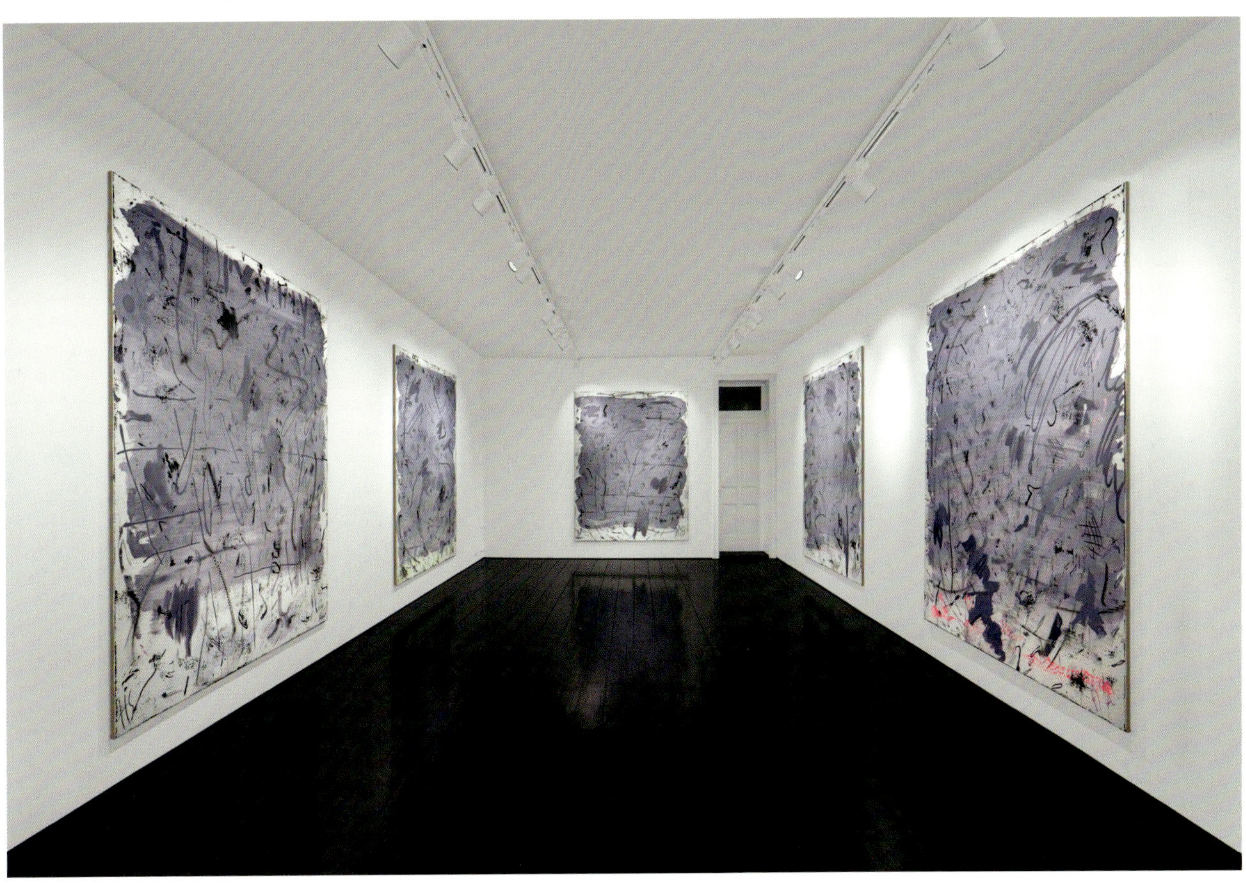

Die Unschuldigen, 2020
Contemporary Fine Arts, Berlin
Foto / photo: Matthias Kolb

Ich habe das Gefühl, dass ich die ganze Zeit immer dach-
te, der „Gegner" oder die „Lösung" ist das Umfeld vom
Bild. Nun stelle ich aber mehr und mehr fest, dass das
vielleicht nicht stimmt und sich tatsächlich alles in dem
Rechteck abspielt. So ganz simpel. Bei der CFA-Show
wollte ich nicht mit Schnullifax überzeugen, sondern mit
den Bildern. Irgendwie alles weglassen, was man in Berlin
als cool empfindet. Ich fand es dadurch dann ehrlich
gesagt ziemlich cool …

**Das ist eben der Punkt. Man muss sich erst mal den Rah-
men schaffen, die Legitimation sozusagen. Aber riskanter
und spannender wird es mit weniger drumherum.**

Das stimmt. Irgendwie ist man halt manchmal so getrieben davon, mithalten zu wollen. Aber als Maler ist man immer gleich hip oder out. Die Grundbedingungen von Malerei ändern sich ja nicht. Das muss man einfach akzeptieren irgendwann. Das hat man neulich auch in Frankfurt gesehen: Du, Jana und ich hingen in der Grässlin-Show, die der Malycha kuratiert hatte, in einer Reihe. Bild an Bild oder Bild gegen Bild. Wie fandest Du das? Wir kennen uns jetzt schon ewig lange und so hat das dann doch noch nie stattgefunden …

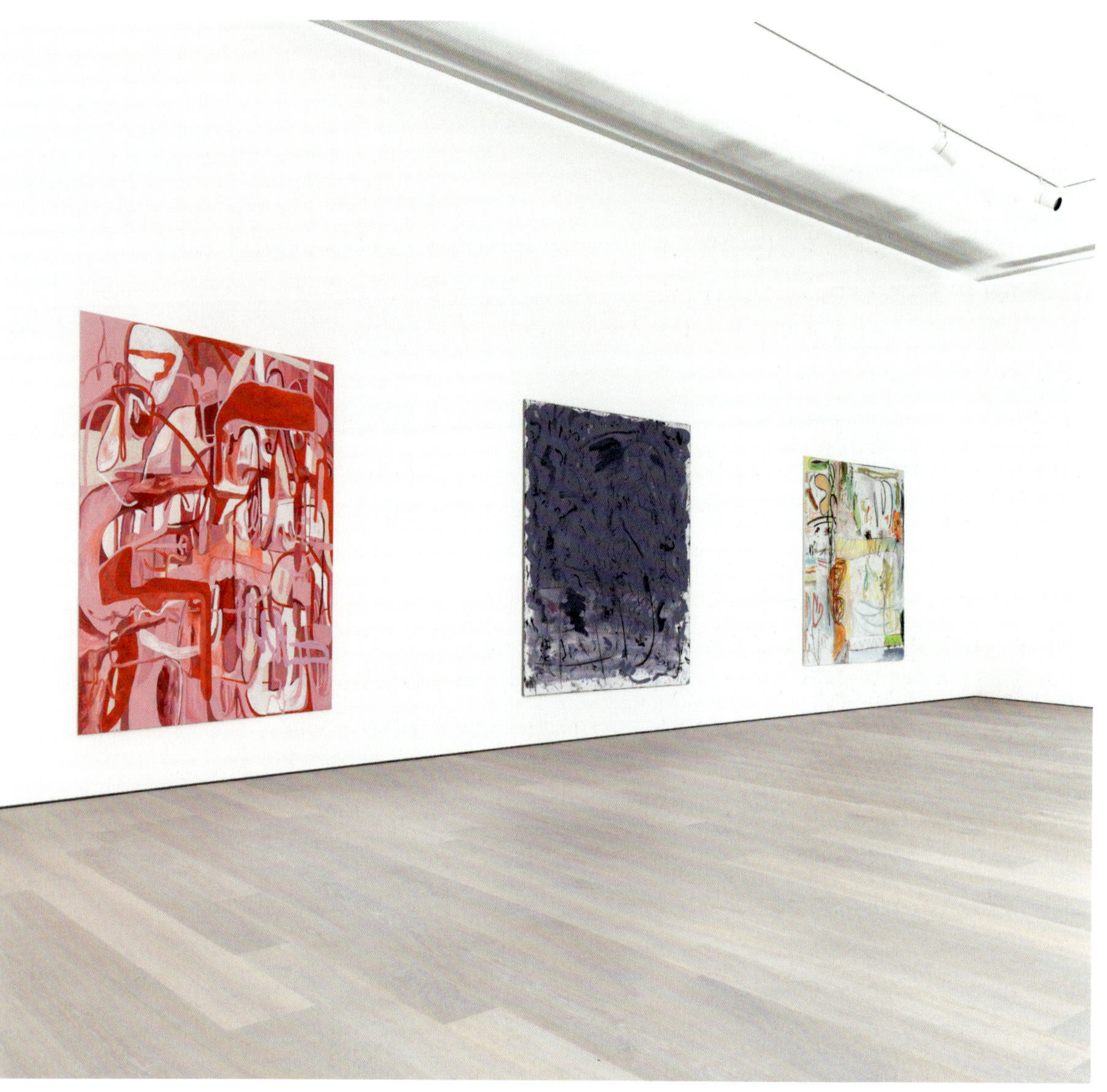

Na, es gab schon ein paar Versuche, die in die Richtung gingen mit uns, aber tatsächlich noch nie so konzentriert. Dort ging es dann um die Competition, über die wir sprachen! Gerade wegen der persönlichen Nähe zueinander und in gewisser Weise auch der Arbeiten. Was CM dort geplant hat, ging auf. Ob die Schau den Diskurs jetzt weiterbringt, weiß ich nicht, aber es wurde ziemlich unverschämt aufgezeigt, was geht.

Echo Chamber, 2020
Jana Schröder, Henning Strassburger,
Andreas Breunig
Galerie Bärbel Grässlin, Frankfurt
Foto / photo: Wolfgang Günzel

Ist für Dich Kunst eigentlich etwas Soziales? Bei Euch zuhause ist immer viel Kunstbesuch, Du und Jana hattet mal einen Raum, der auch nur Wettbewerbe veranstaltet hat, oder jetzt in Heppenheim sollten die Leute Tischtennis gegeneinander spielen und wieder gab es etwas zu gewinnen: Ein Bild von Dir. Nur hat das niemand gewonnen, weil Du so gut spielst, dass keiner an Dich rankam. Aber das Soziale ist doch irgendwie auch auffällig?

Ich denke Kunst hat grundsätzlich eine gesellschaftliche Aufgabe zu leisten. Ich habe im Gespräch mit CM für das Magazin zur KVHP-Ausstellung schon gesagt, dass Kunst, die sich nur um sich selbst dreht, überflüssig ist. Es ist toll, sich mit Fachleuten über die Arbeit zu streiten, aber man hat doch den Wunsch, alle mitzunehmen. Wenn man beim Tischtennisturnier eine Arbeit gewinnen kann, ist das doch erstmal super. In unserem Offspace, der GSK, hatten wir ja die Biertombola. Das war noch extremer, da musste man so gar nichts leisten. Bier trinken und Arbeit gewinnen. Also um den Bogen zu Deiner Frage zurück zu spannen: Ohne Austausch und Diskurs kommt weder der Künstler noch die Gesellschaft weiter. Das ist alles sozial und muss im öffentlichen Raum stattfinden. Das wirst Du doch auch unterschreiben. Als Dirigent Deiner Blaskapelle, Betreiber vom Beach Office und und und … überall gehst Du auf die Audience zu.

Ich bin halt zusätzlich auch noch 'ne Rampensau. Da ich nur schwer mit dem Alleinsein im Atelier umgehen kann, treiben meine anderen Projekte manchmal eigenartig soziale Blüten. Ich sehe mich schon als Kommunikator, deswegen will ich auch, dass meine Bilder etwas Erzählerisches haben. Sie sind eigentlich nicht formal, würde ich sagen. Wobei … das ist auch eine schwierige Aussage.

Du hast Dich oft mit dem Konsum von Kultur und der Fragwürdigkeit dessen auseinandergesetzt, immer von innen heraus. Würdest du sagen, dass

es einen Effekt hatte, sowohl auf Dich als auch auf zumindest einige Rezipienten?

Ich sehe „Kunst" als ein offenes System. Das heißt, auch als Künstler bin ich ja Kunst-Konsument. Wenn ich einen Schauspieler oder Autor kennenlerne, bin ich natürlich selber fasziniert und will an dieses System andocken. Da brennen mir richtig die Synapsen durch vor Freude an Möglichkeiten. Und die gleiche Möglichkeit, an mein System anzudocken, will ich anderen bieten. Manche nutzen das rücksichtslos aus, mit anderen macht es mehr Spaß. Gleichzeitig sehe ich auch die Chance, bei Ausstellungen wie in Heppenheim, also quasi auf dem Land, mit Leuten in Kontakt zu treten. Plötzlich ist da viel mehr möglich als in der Großstadt zum Beispiel, weil die Leute das Angebot ganz anders annehmen. Auch kritischer.

Die Nummer hier wird gerade ein bisschen zu tiefsinnig. Und das auf so eine dreist oberflächliche Art. Lass' mal über unser Lieblings-Weingut aus Heppenheim plaudern: Ich bin voll auf Freiberger! Und Du?

Ganz ehrlich, Andi, der KVHP-Vorstand, Mona, Bernd, Anke, Uwe und Uli, die begrüßen einen schon am Bahnhof mit vollen Flaschen Schampus. Ich habe jeweils nur Erinnerungen an diese ersten Flaschen, danach ist alles verschwommen. Ich bewundere, dass Du jetzt auf Feinschmecker machen willst, nur wüsste ich nicht, was ich später so alles getrunken habe. Wie ich schon am Anfang sagte: Der Kunstverein liefert die Eskalation gleich mit.

Also auch Freiberger …

ANDREAS BREUNIG

**Know what I consider to be an absolute quality of KVHP?
The absolute madness that prevails there. Good dynamics.
You've already knocked one out in 2011 – "Softidrink"! –,
right at the beginning. Have they always been like that?**

HENNING STRASSBURGER

Back then, the crazy thing was, I didn't know what was
going on. Actually, the organizers themselves pushed for a
certain escalation. Thus, the surprise effect was consider-
able. Usually, escalation is expected of the artists. Here,
the Kunstverein itself delivers it right away. Rather unique,
I'd say. Maybe that's why you always come up with something special. For example, in Heppenheim both of us pre-
sented painting in a more installative way. Was it due to
the space or to us? Why can't we just hang the paintings
on the wall?

**I guess, the space accommodates our formal ideas of presentation.
Particularly, as your concepts often revolve around the question of
how painting can operate in the context of present-day media consumption. For this, a wall is not really necessary. Or am I wrong?
And besides, at KVHP paintings on the wall just look crappy.**

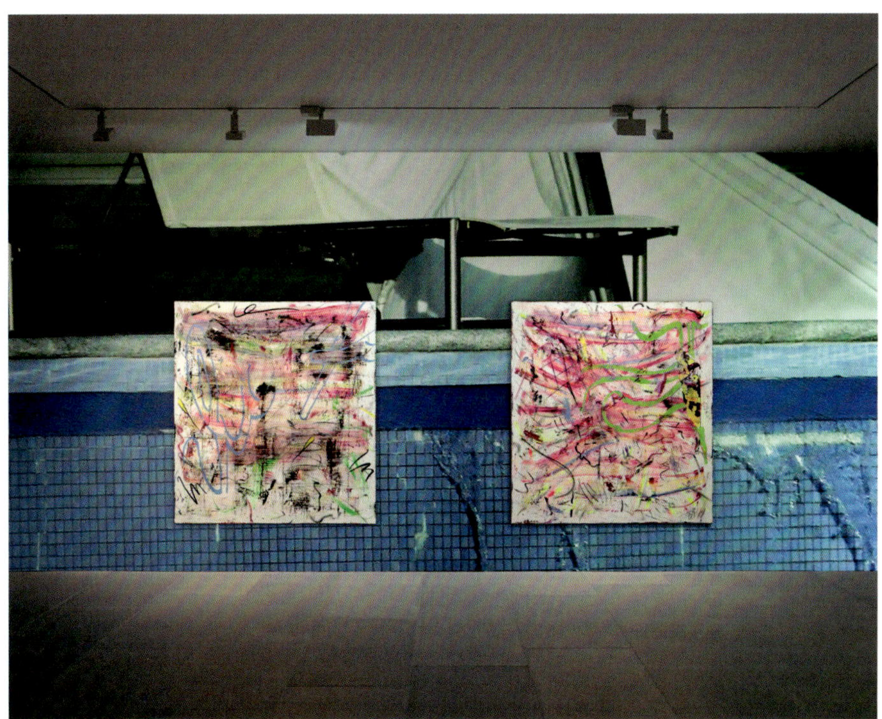

KARMA MANSION, 2019
Blain|Southern, London
Foto / photo: Peter Mallet

True, the shabby wallpaper
simply won't accept any
painting upon itself. So, this
time I thought I'd place the
paintings as a sort of display
panels right in the middle of
the space. Together with the
misprinted wallpapers of my
2019 London show "Karma
Mansion". In Heppenheim,
the prior ambience of the
paintings now became a
painterly object in itself. To
me it worked out quite well.

Together with Jana, you orga-
nized a competitive tournament in Heppenheim and plastered the
city with election posters and one could choose who the winner

should be. Since you were the winner, your prize was making the show "Play me / Have no Probs". Where does the hunt for the thrill of being the winner stem from? Does painting = winning?

Well, we'd chosen this form of battle to create spatial objectivity. By means of massive contextual subjectivity. For me, painting is more about avoiding failure. If you have to win for that, fine. But seriously, where is the opponent? The competition is always with one's own self. Sure, I go to Heppenheim and tell myself in advance: "My show has to be a bigger banger than Hennich's." But after all, both were great, weren't they?

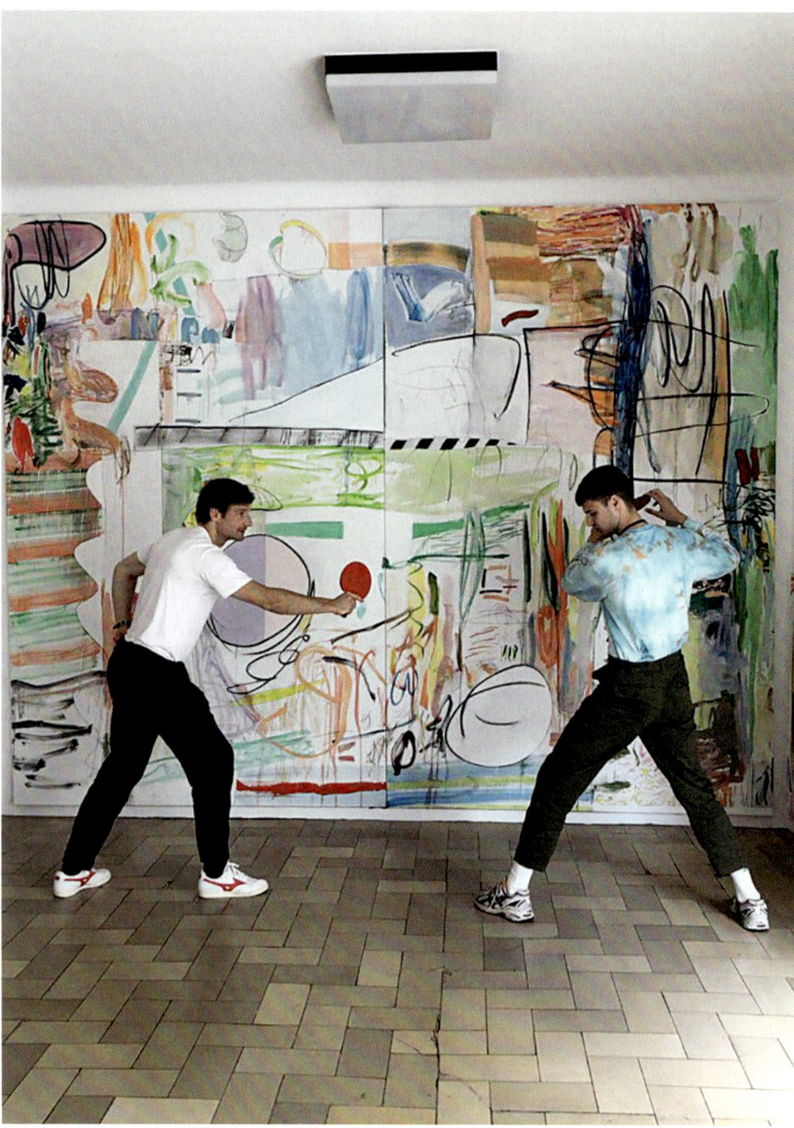

Zu Besuch im / on a visit at Kunstverein, 2020
Foto / photo: Uwe Emig

Totally, I even went back there to play a little game of table tennis amidst your installation. And suddenly everything clicked: painting as an advertising banner. Self-advertising, so to say. But I must admit I'm always aware of the competition. That's why my show was called "ALPHAKEVIN", quite the blunt territorial attitude.

By the way, I noticed in your last exhibitions you allowed for more panel painting (uhh, the word is horrible). Especially at CFA's, top pictures. Do you eventually have to face the core problems once you've reached your mid-thirties? That's a question which currently drives me.

Assumedly, I always thought that the context is the "opponent" or the "solution" of the image. But now, I gradually realize that this

18

might not be the case and that everything is actually happening within this odd rectangle. Quite simply. For the CFA show I didn't want to convince with fancy bits and pieces but with genuine paintings. In fact, by means of leaving out everything that is considered cool in Berlin. And to be honest, I found it pretty cool …

That's just the point. You have to create a certain referential framework, at first, the so-called legitimation. But then everything gets riskier and more exciting, the less fuzz you make about it.

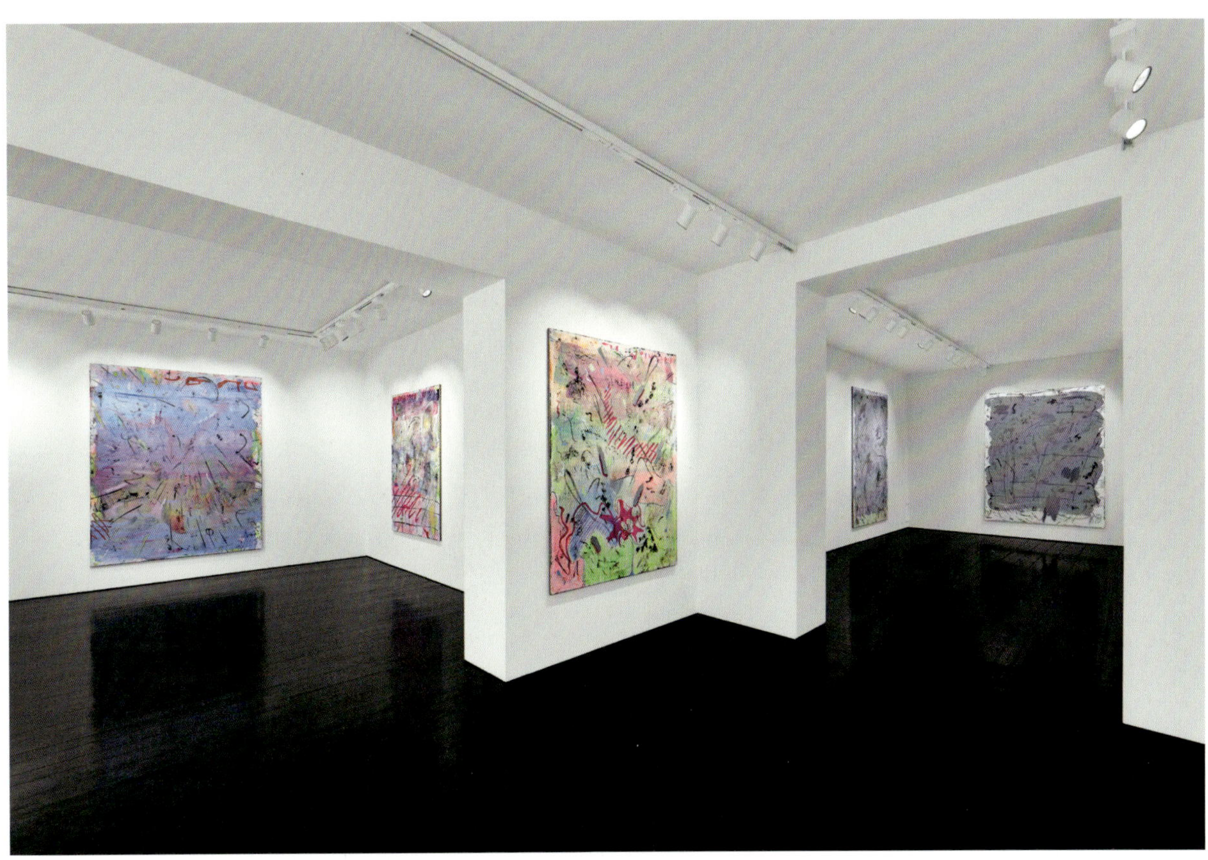

Die Unschuldigen, 2020
Contemporary Fine Arts, Berlin
Foto / photo: Matthias Kolb

Right. At times, one's so driven by the desire to keep up, somehow. Only, as a painter you're either instantly hip or just out. Still, the basic conditions of painting do not change. At one point, you have to accept them. Take Frankfurt for example: You, Jana and I hung next to each other in that group show Malycha had curated at Bärbel Grässlin's. Painting next to painting or painting against painting. How did you like that? We have known each other for such a long time and still, such a thing has never happened before …

Well, there were a few attempts involving us that aimed for that but never this focussed. It was exactly about

19

**the competition we talked about! Even more so due to
the personal closeness to each other and, in a certain
way, the works. What CM had planned worked out.
I'm not sure how the show will continue the discourse
but, anyhow, it has shown quite impudently what is
possible.**

In your book, is art something social? You're always host-
ing a lot of arty visitors, together with Jana you ran a space
which exclusively organized competitions, in Heppenheim
people were supposed to play table tennis against each
other and once more there was something to win: one of
your paintings. However, nobody won it. You play so well
that nobody could beat you. But isn't the social also some-
what suspicious?

**Fundamentally, art has a social task to perform, I think. In the
conversation with CM for my KVHP magazine, I already said that
art which is only concerned with itself is superfluous. Expert ar-
guments are great fun but the desire to inspire everyone remains.
Thus, being able to win an artwork at a table tennis tournament
 is great in itself. Back at our offspace, the GSK, we had the beer
raffle which was even more extreme. You didn't have to do any-
thing except drinking beer to win a piece. But to get back to your
question: Without exchange and discourse neither the artist nor
society can move forward. Everything is social and has to take
place in public space. You'll sign that, won't you. Conducting your
own brass band, co-operating the Beach Office and and and ...
everywhere you're appealing to an audience.**

And on top of that, I am quite the spotlight hog-
ger. As I find it difficult to deal with being alone
in the studio, my other projects sometimes bring
about peculiar social blossoms. I consider myself being a communicator and explicitly want
my paintings to have narrative qualities. They
are not too formal, I'd say. Even though ... that's
a complicated statement as well.

**In all its dubiousness, you've often dealt with the consumption
of culture, always from the inside. Would you say that this had
an effect, both on you and on at least some recipients?**

I see "art" as an open system. Meaning, even as an artist I am an art consumer. When I meet an actor or author, I am naturally fascinated myself and want to dock to this system. My synapses burn out with joy at the possibilities. And I want to offer others the same possibilities to dock to my system. Some people ruthlessly take advantage of this, with others it's more fun. At the same time, I also see the opportunity to get in touch with people at exhibitions like in Heppenheim, I'd say, in the countryside. There, much more is possible than, for example, in a big city, because people accept the offer in a completely different way. More critical, too.

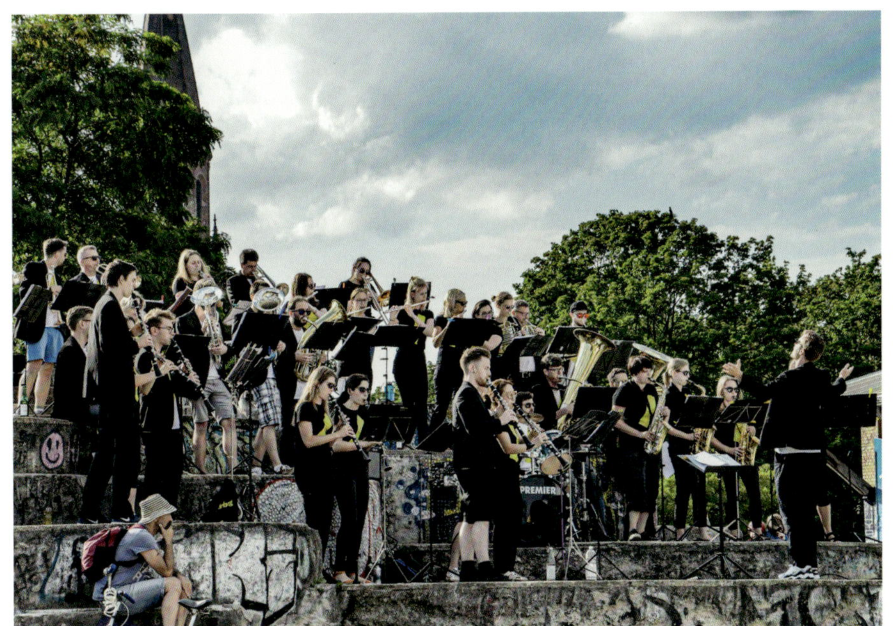

JEB-Band im / at Görlitzer Park Berlin, 2019
Foto / photo: Helge Hemme

This number here is just getting profoundly too deep. That is in such a blunt and superficial way. So, let's chat about our favorite Heppenheim vineyard: I'm all for Freiberger! And you?

Honestly, Andi, the KVHP board, Anke, Uwe, Mona, Bernd and Uli, they greet you at the station with full bottles of champagne. I only have memories of these first bottles, afterwards everything gets blurry. Even if I admire your wilful air of being a gourmet now, I wouldn't know what I drank later. As I said: The Kunstverein provides the escalation right from the start.

So, Freiberger after all …

Splash VI, 2018
200 x 150 cm
Öl auf Leinwand / oil on canvas
Foto / photo: Nick Ash

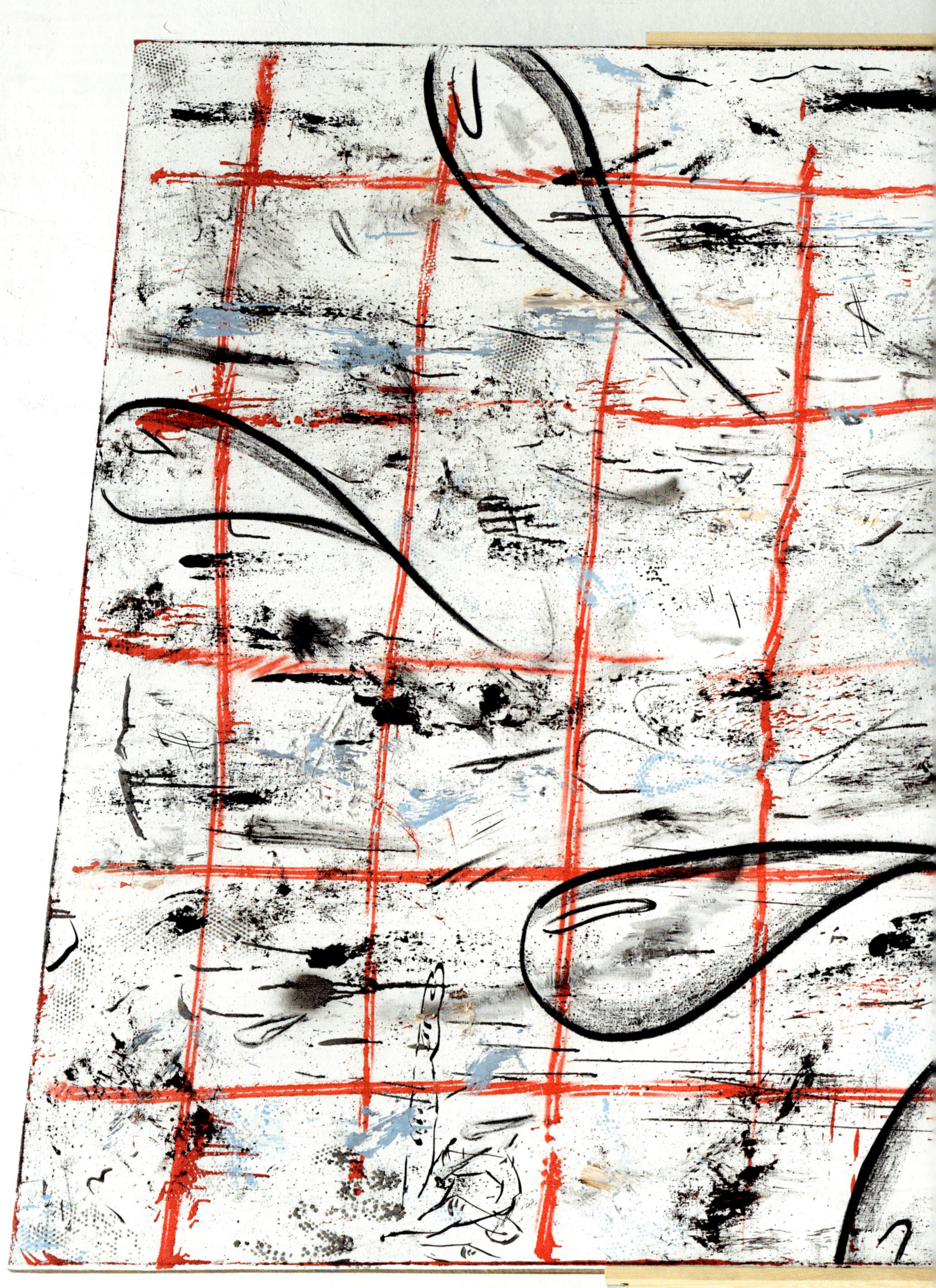

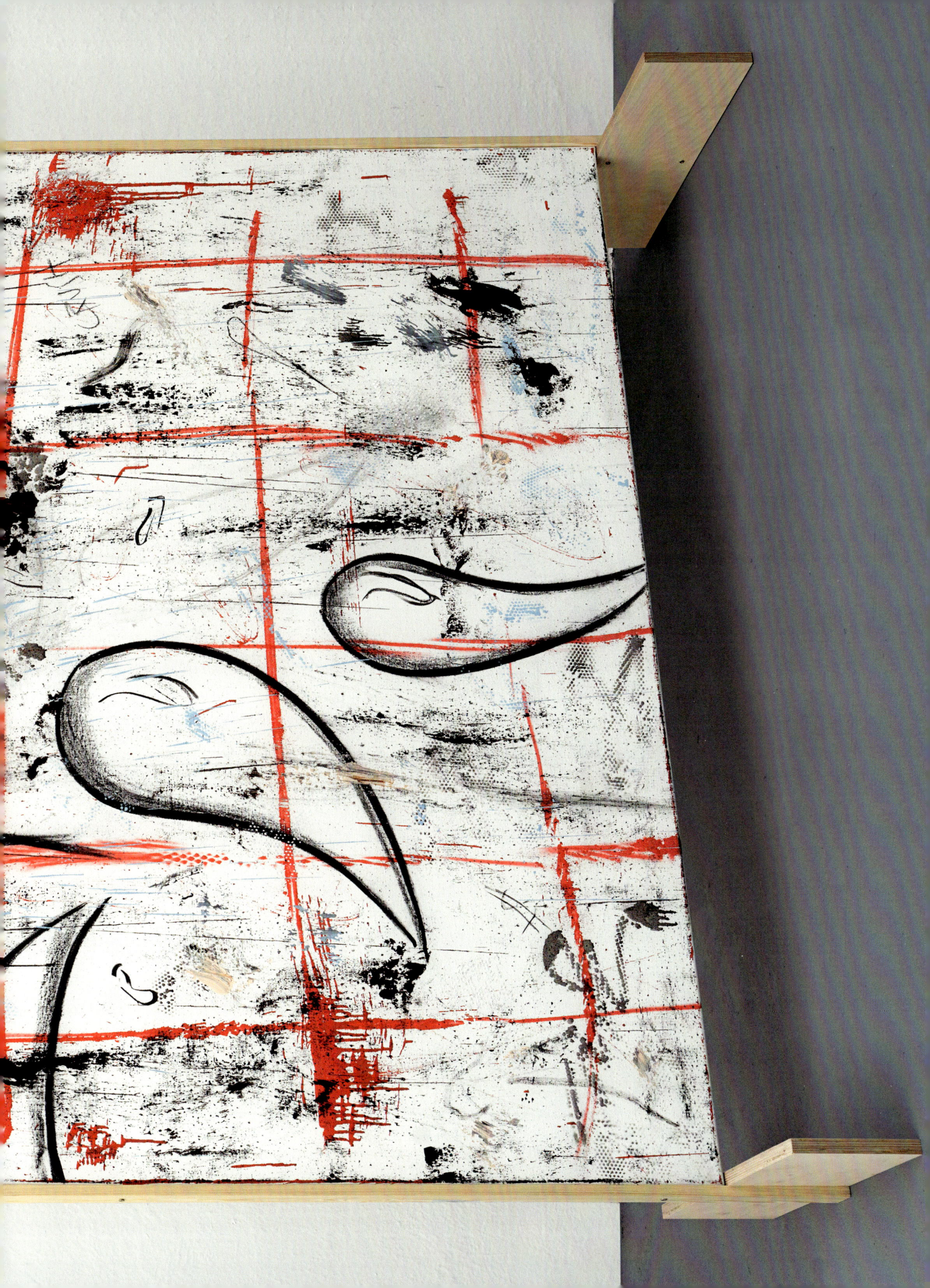

Splash III, 2018
200 x 150 cm
Öl auf Leinwand / oil on canvas
Foto / photo: Trevor Good

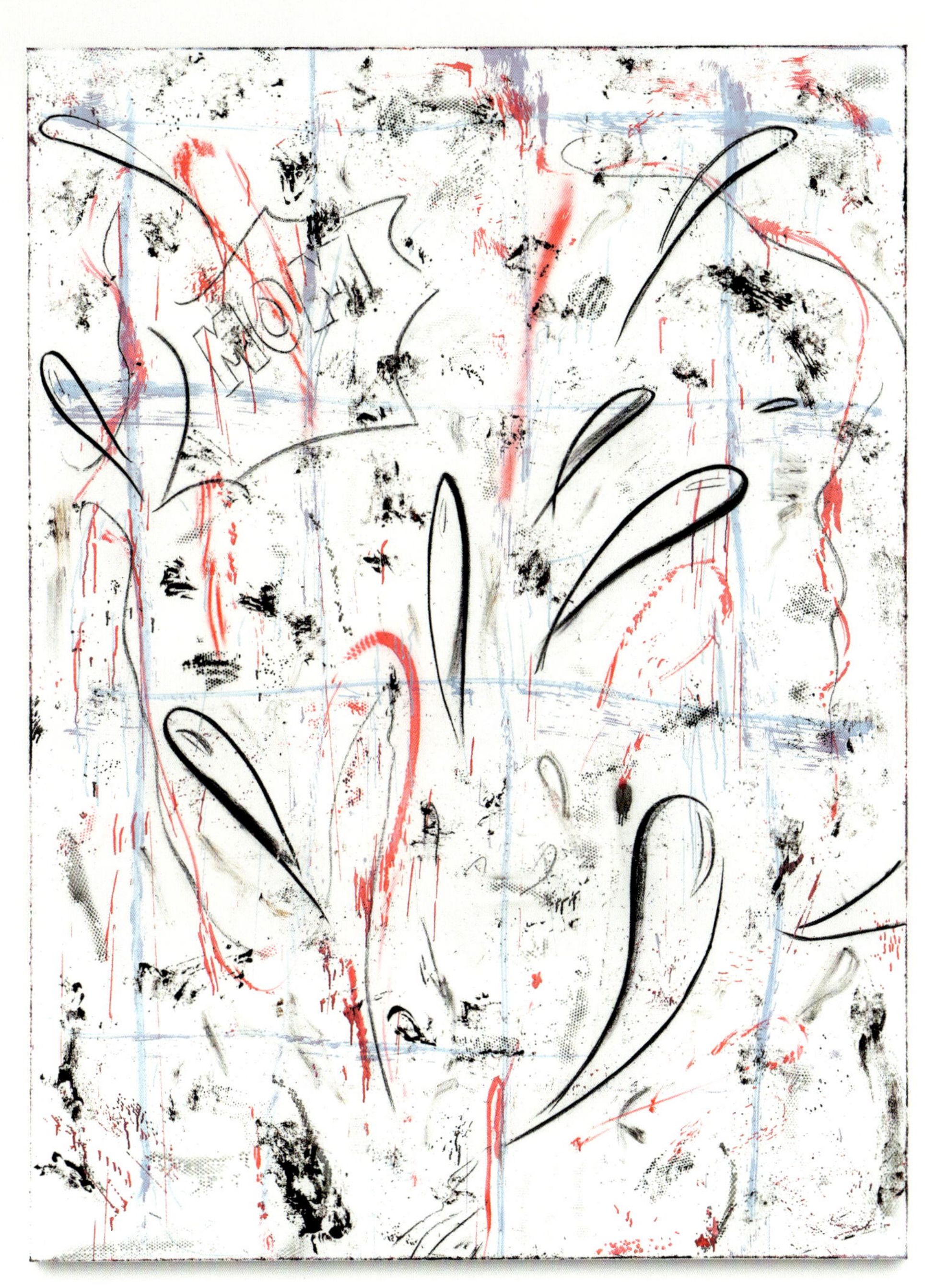
MOM

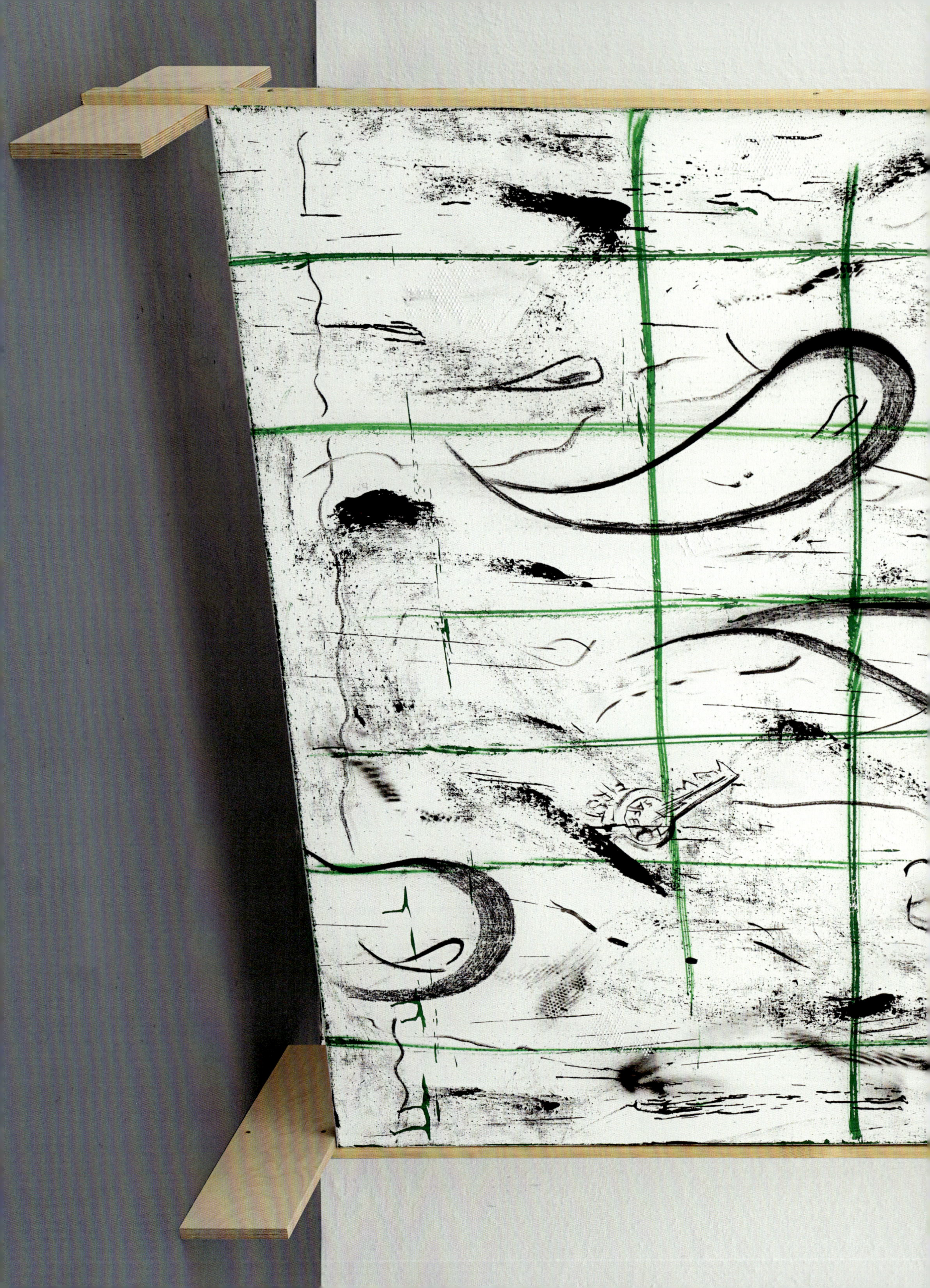

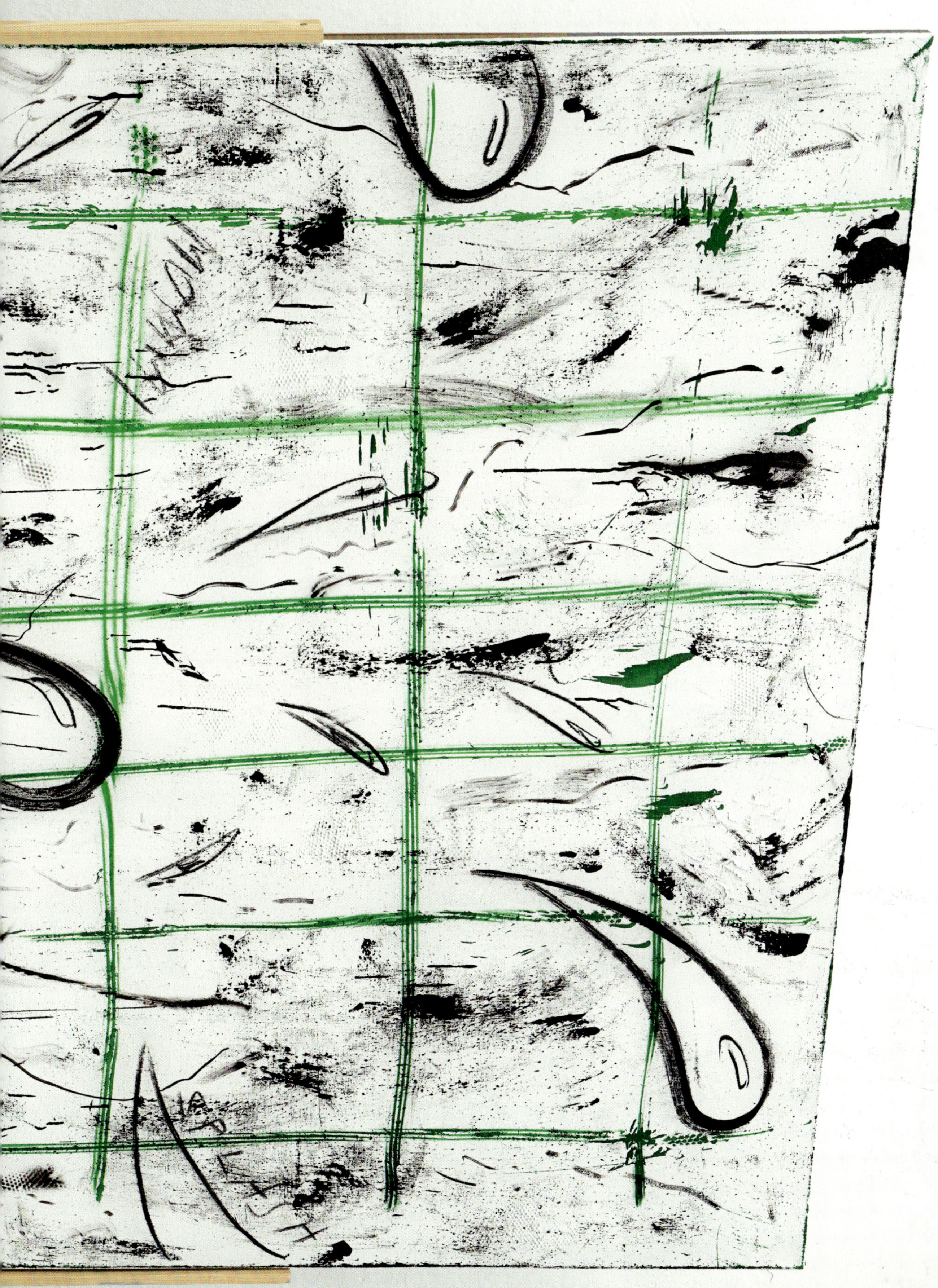

Splash IV, 2018
200 x 150 cm
Öl auf Leinwand / oil on canvas
Foto / photo: Nick Ash

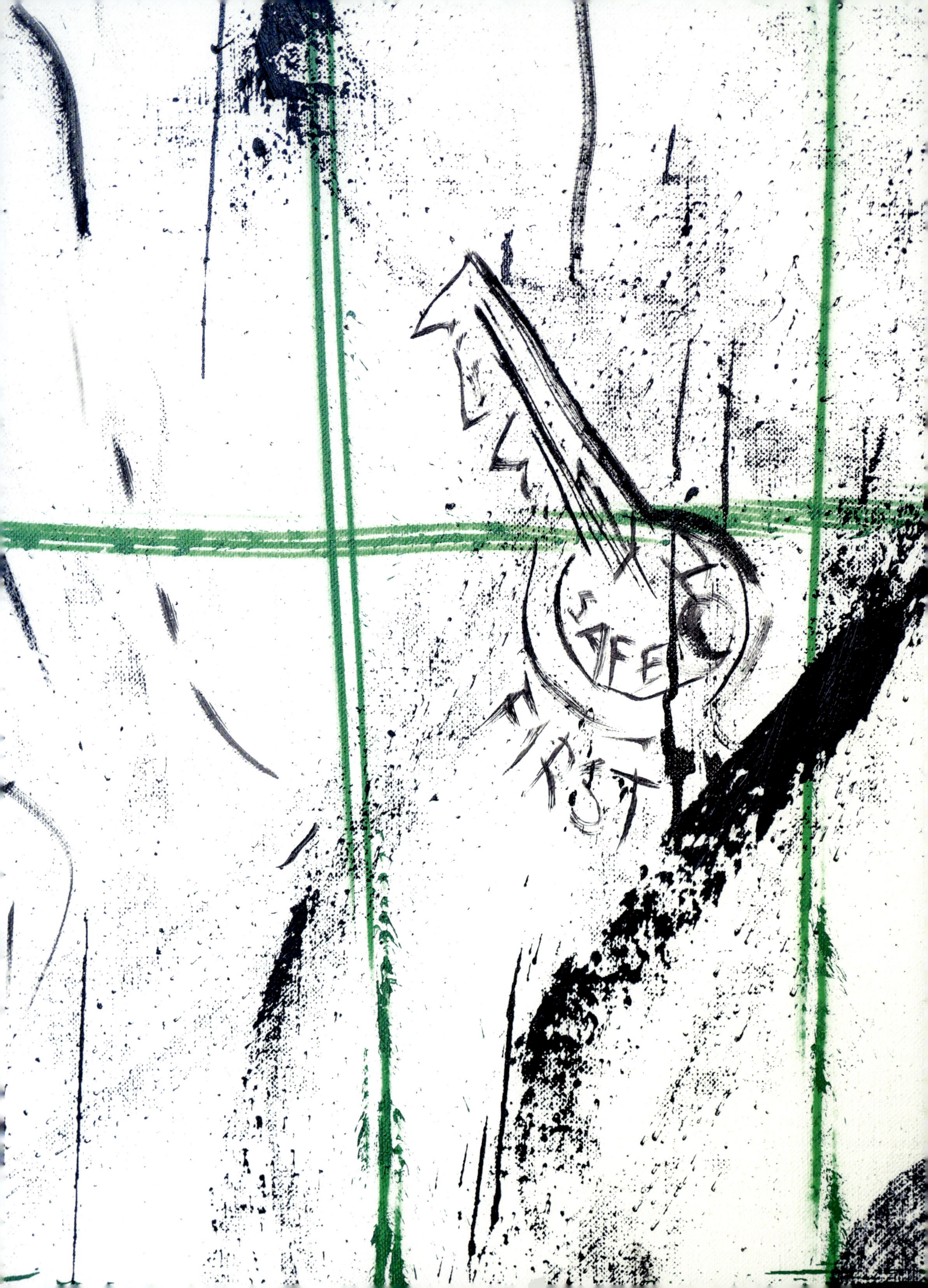

SAFE
FIRST

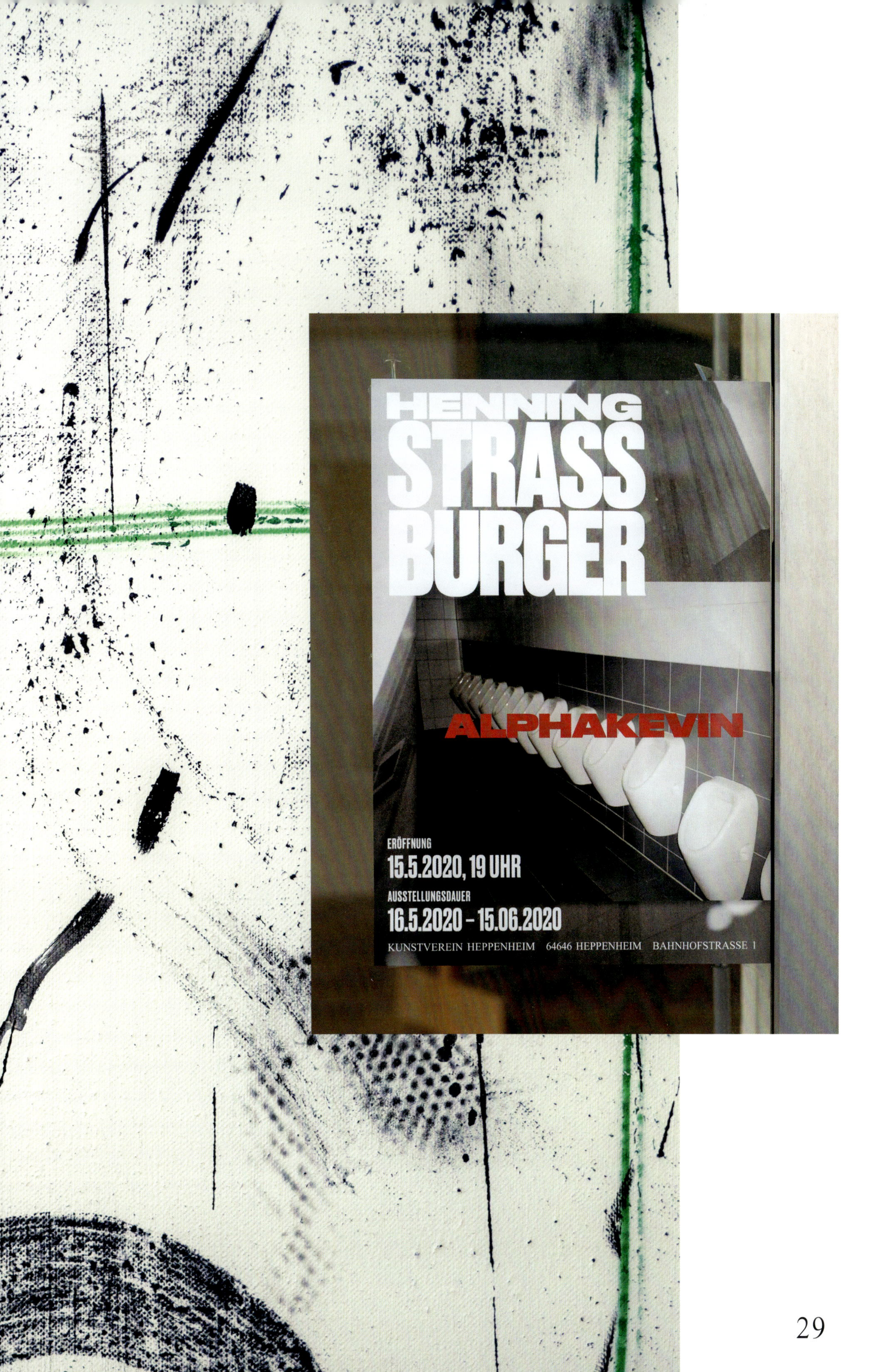

HENNING
STRASS
BURGER
ALPHAKEVIN
ERÖFFNUNG
15.5.2020, 19 UHR
AUSSTELLUNGSDAUER
16.5.2020 – 15.06.2020
KUNSTVEREIN HEPPENHEIM   64646 HEPPENHEIM   BAHNHOFSTRASSE 1

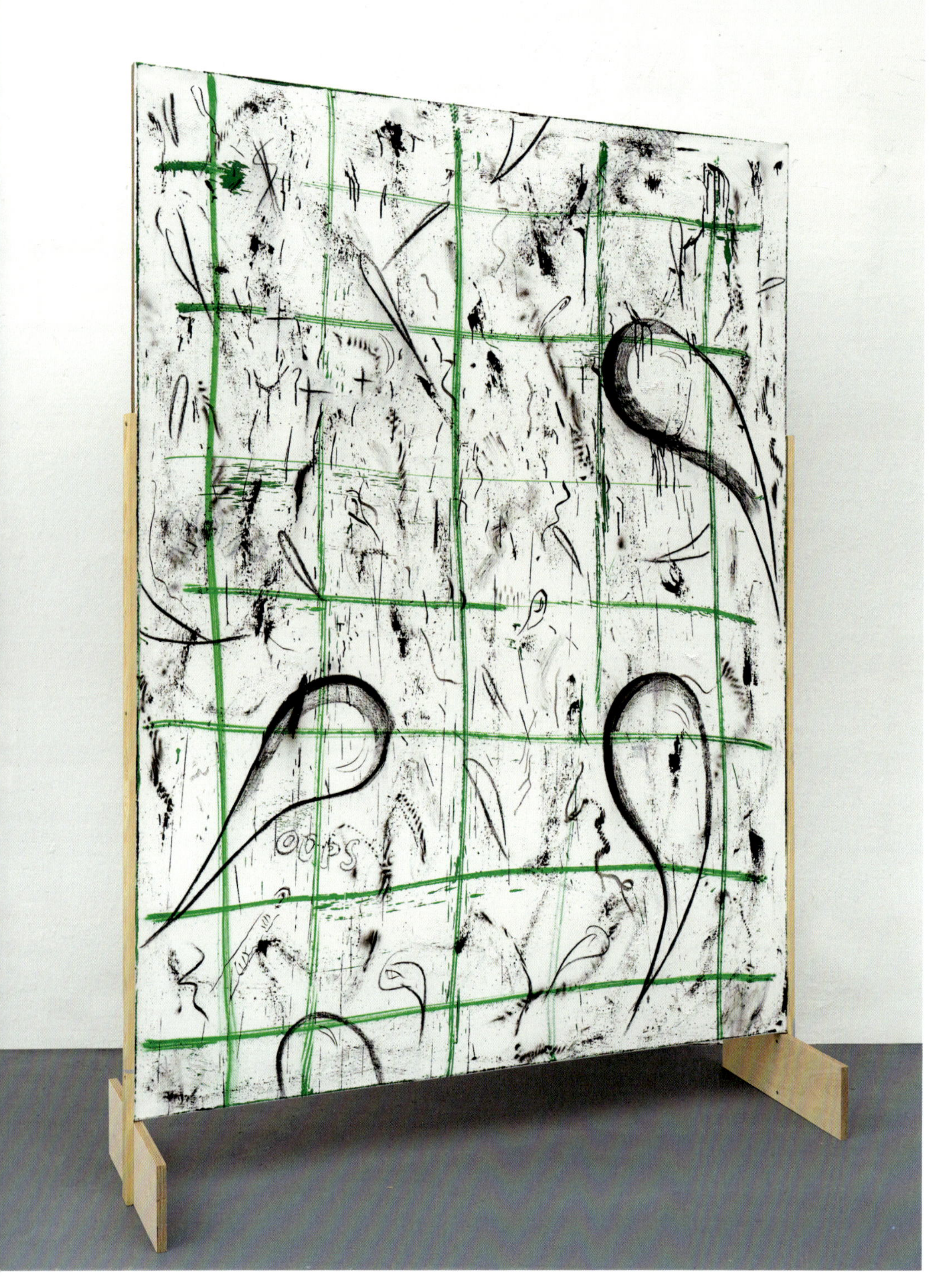

Splash V, 2018
200 x 150 cm
Öl auf Leinwand / oil on canvas
Foto / photo: Nick Ash

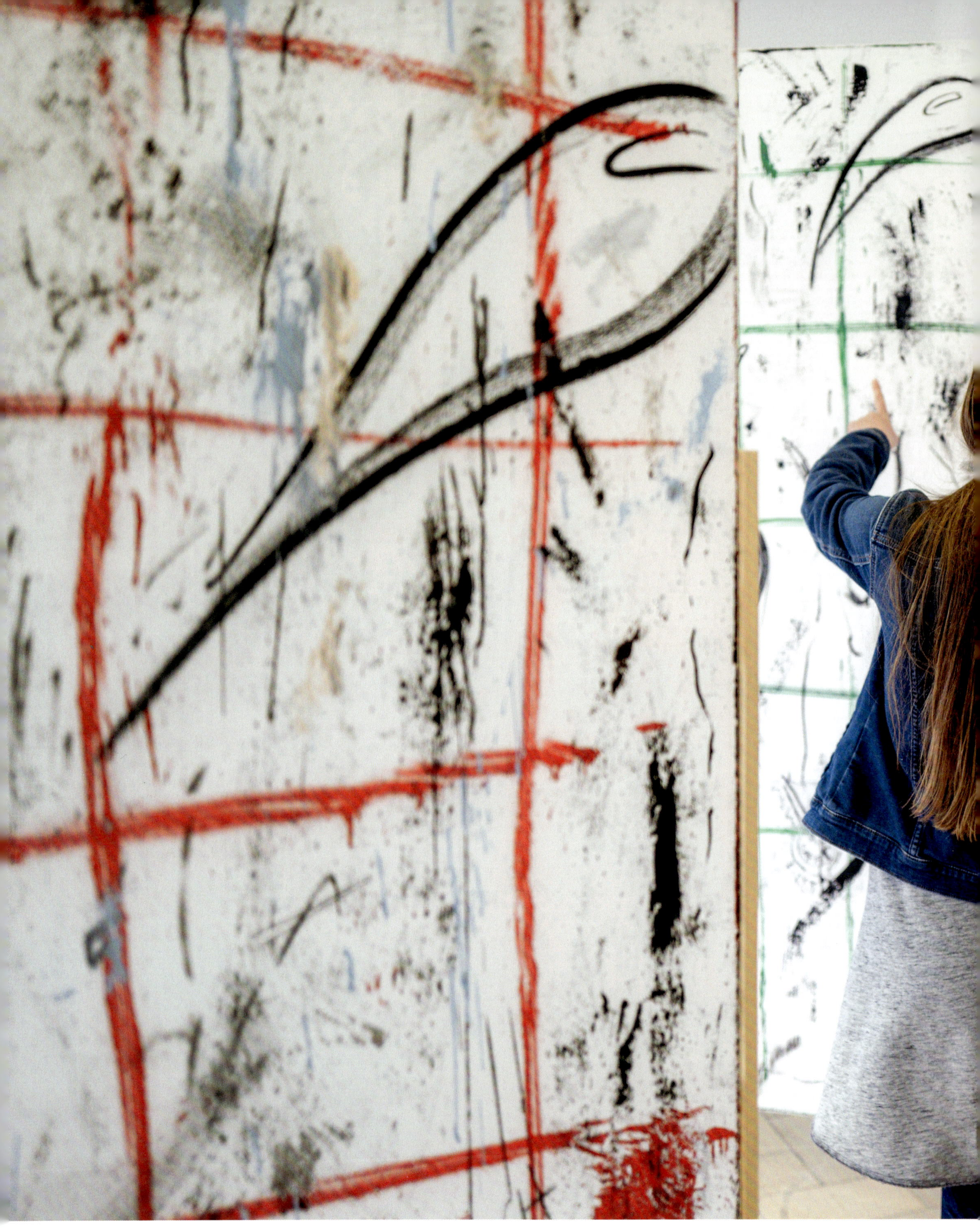

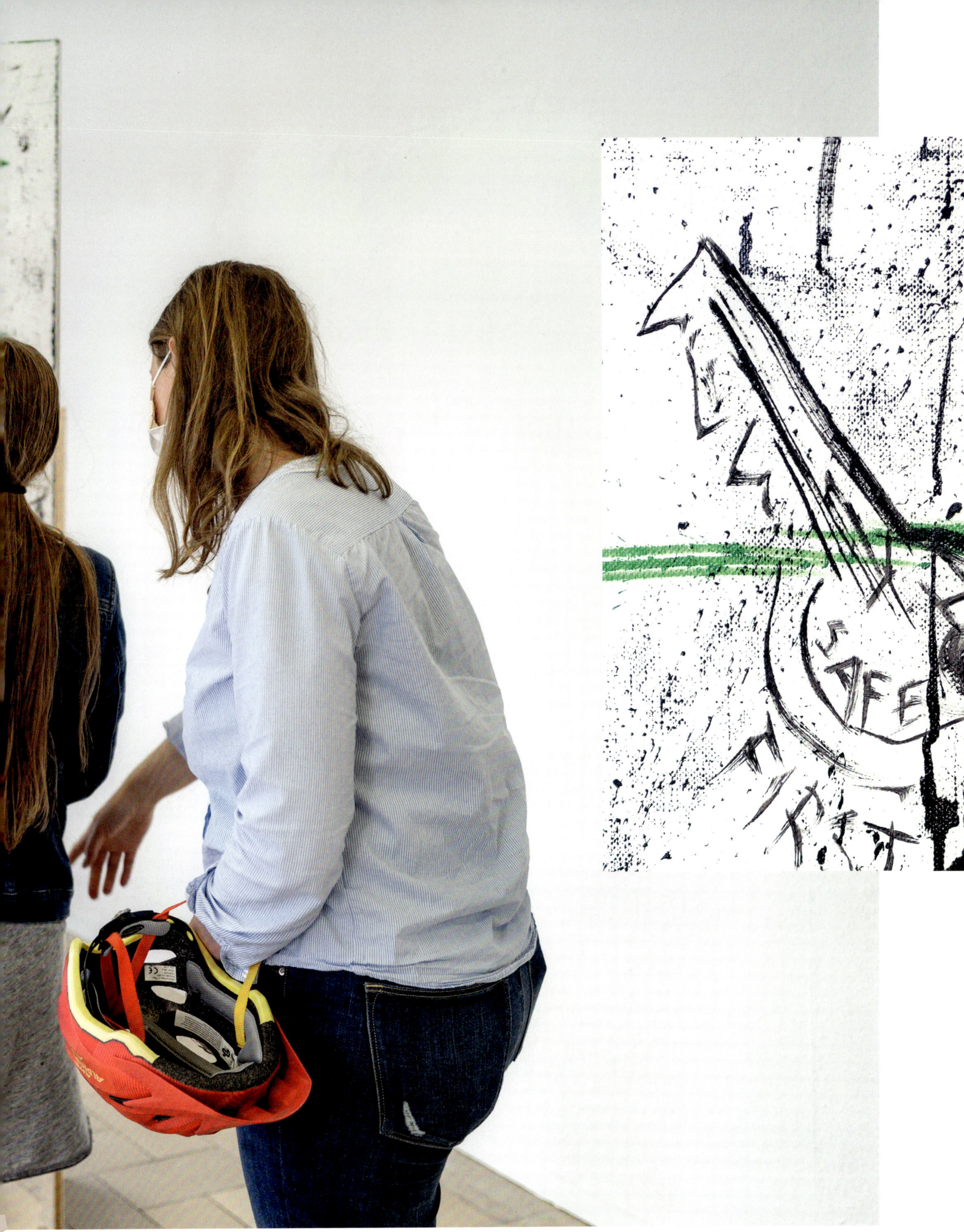

SAFE

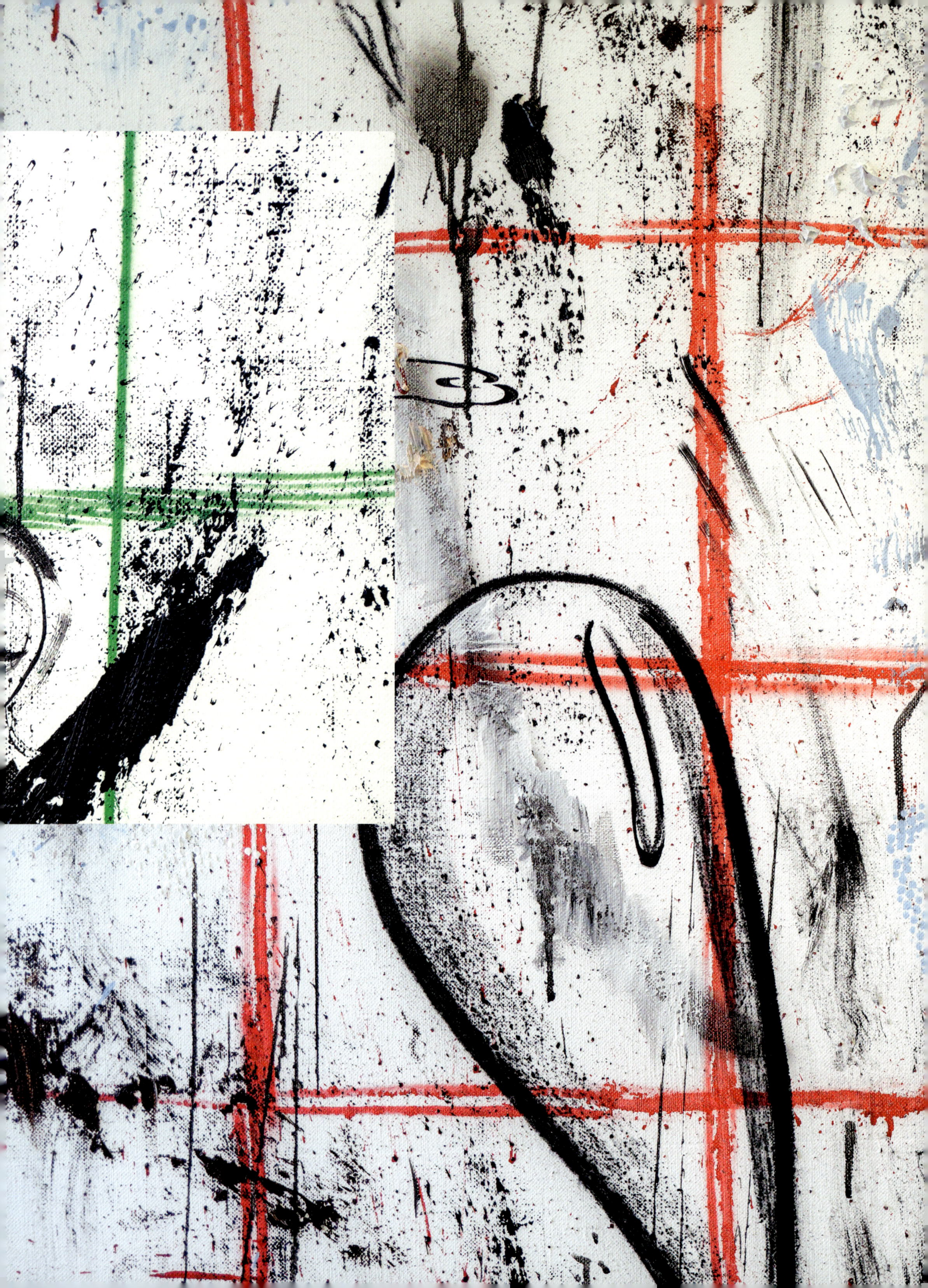

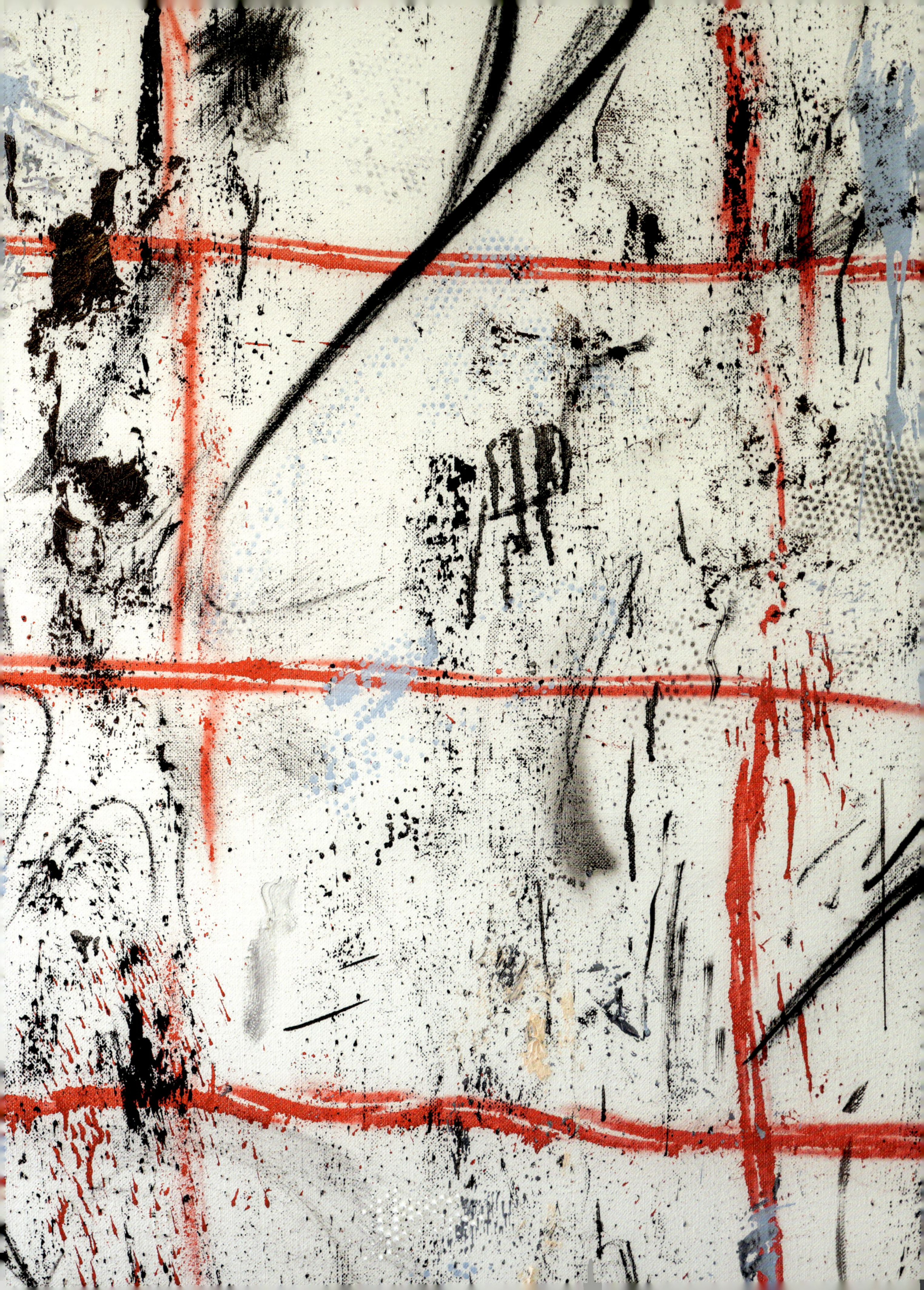

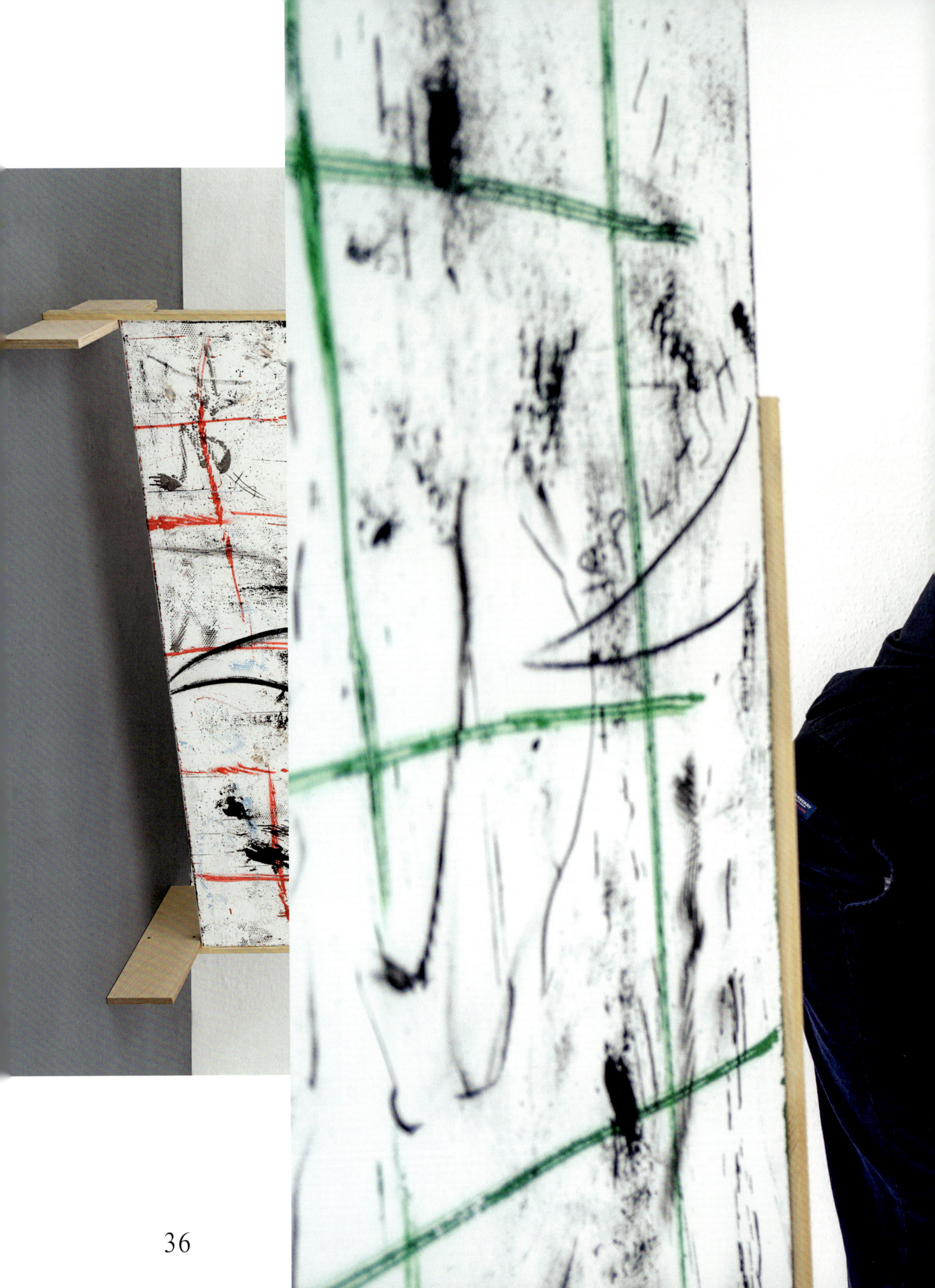

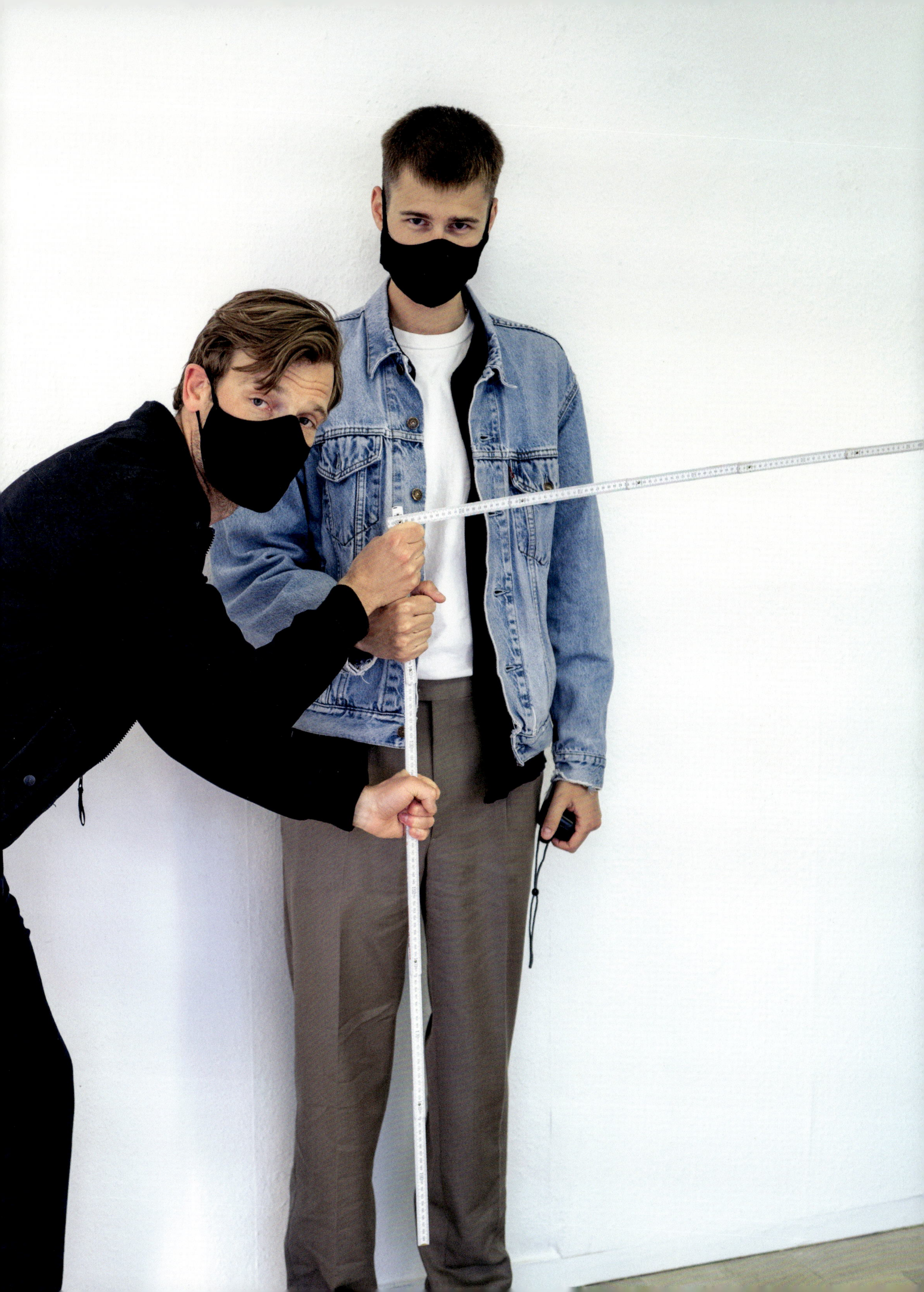

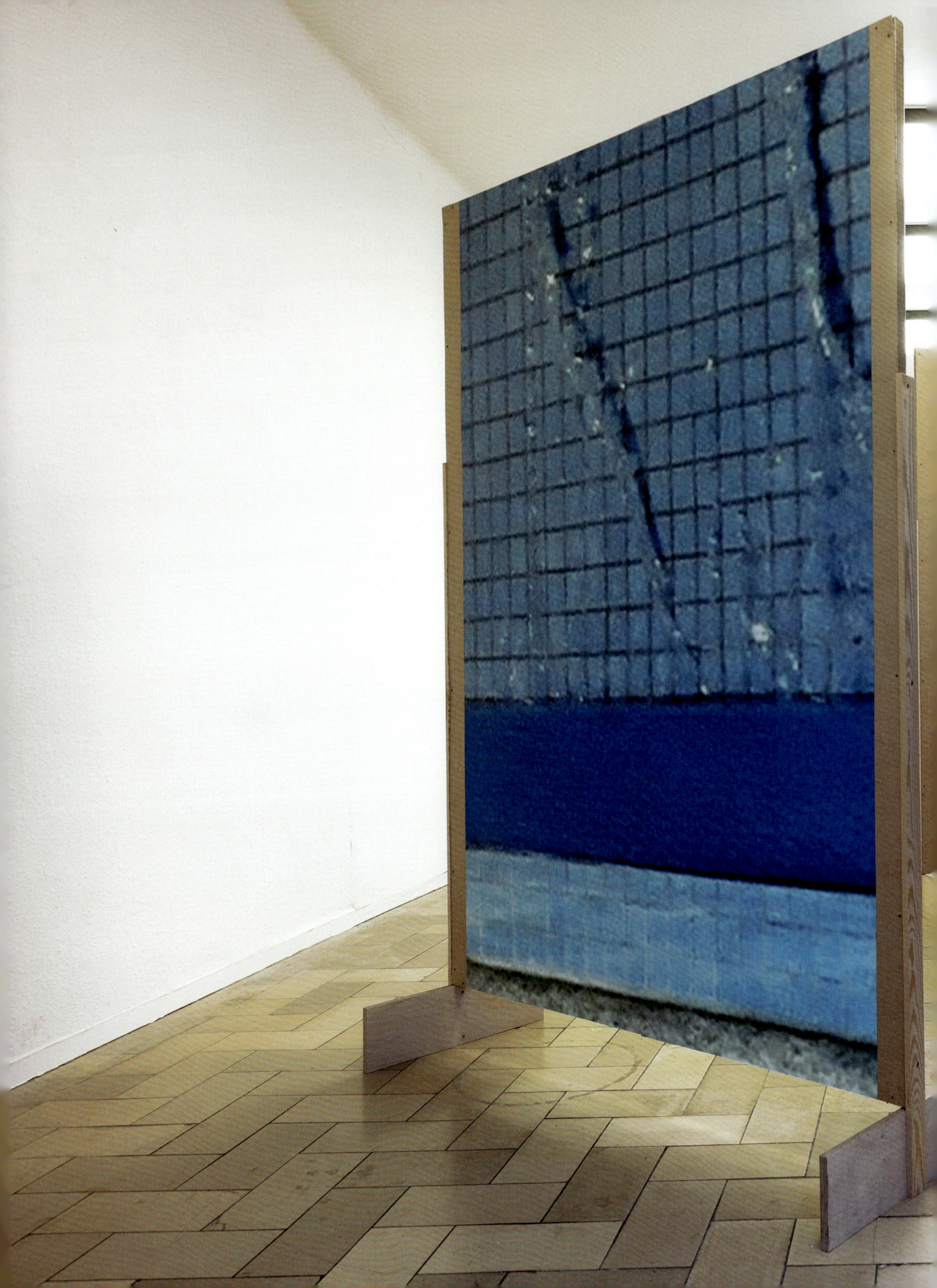

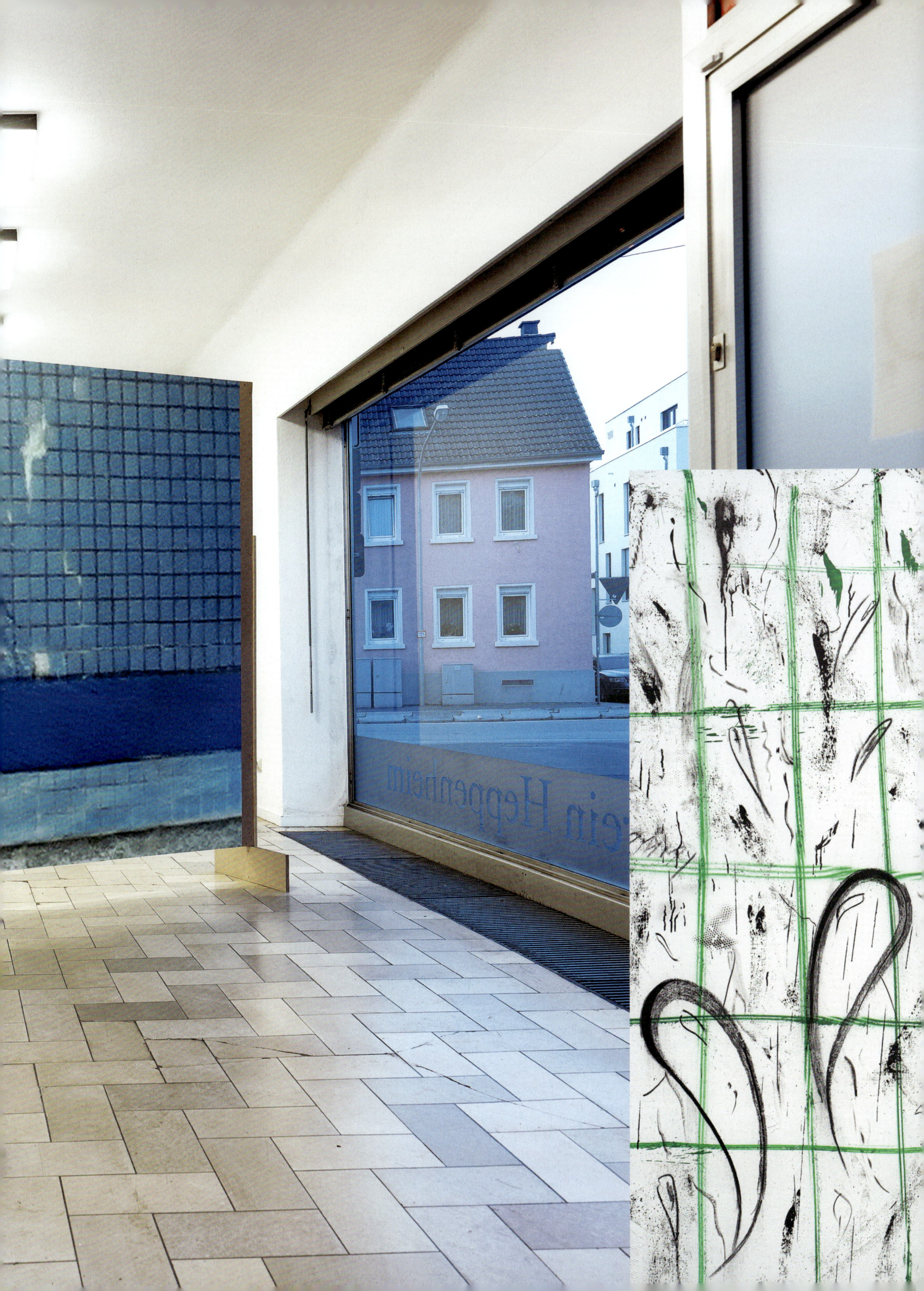

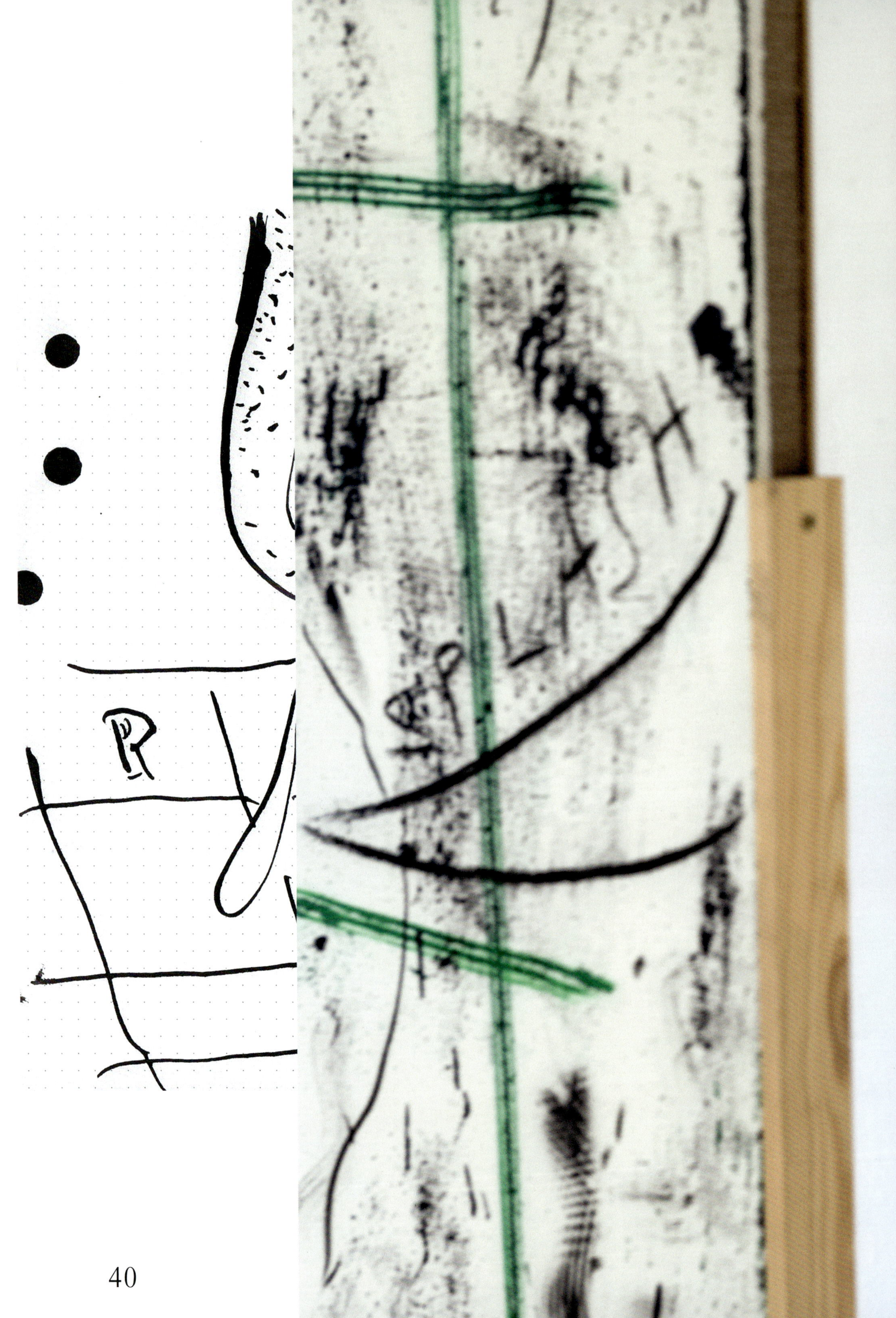

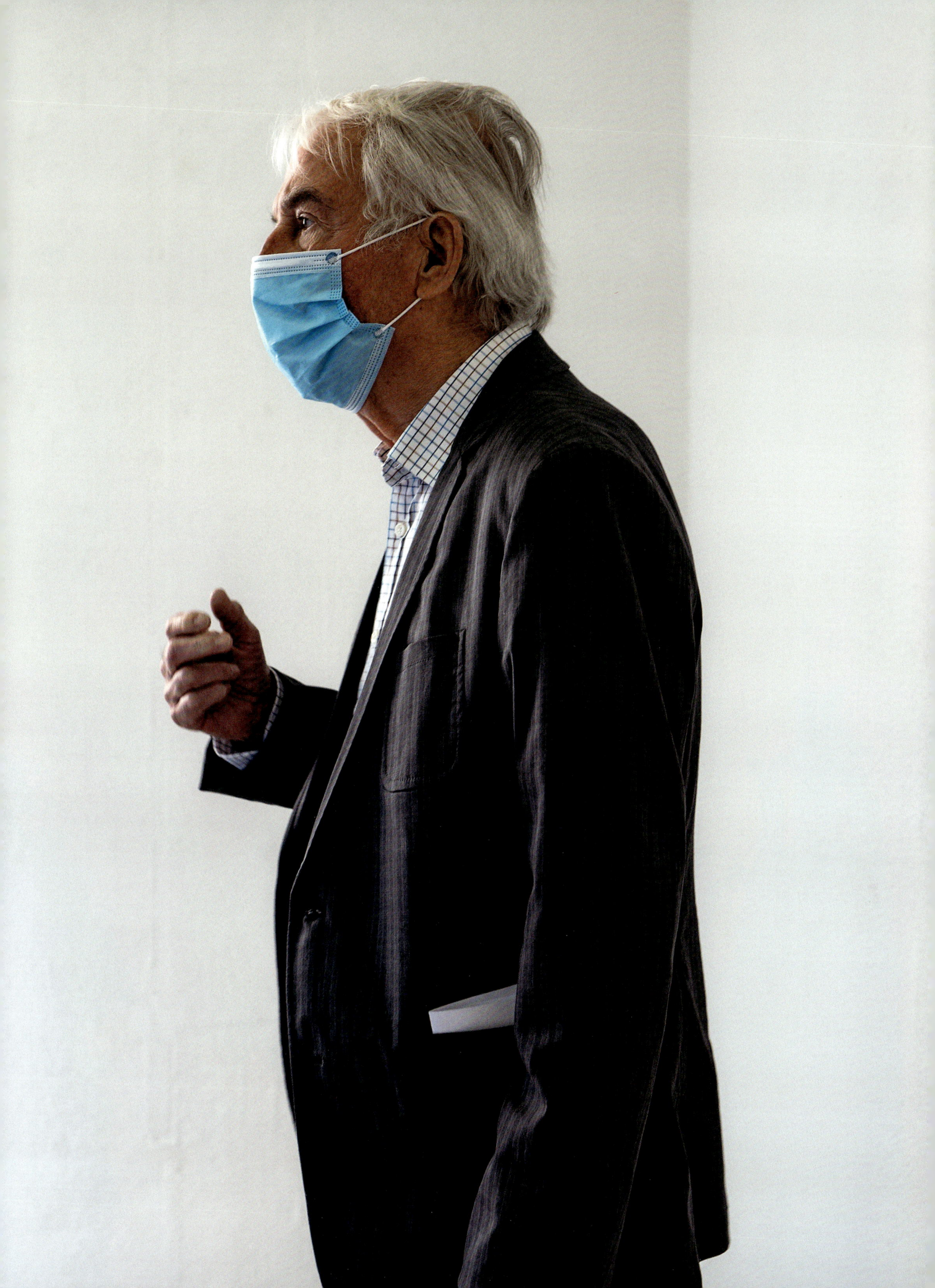

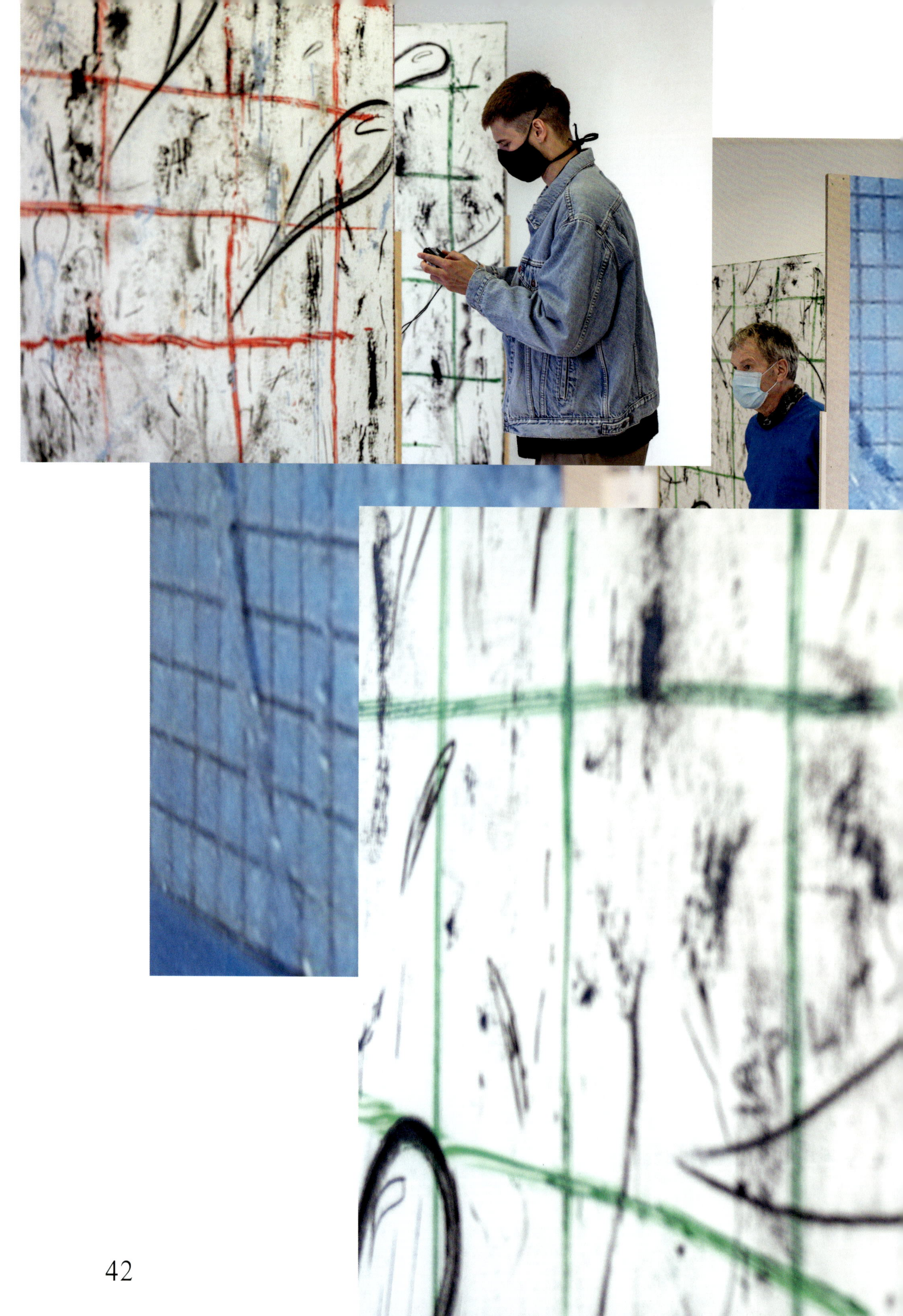

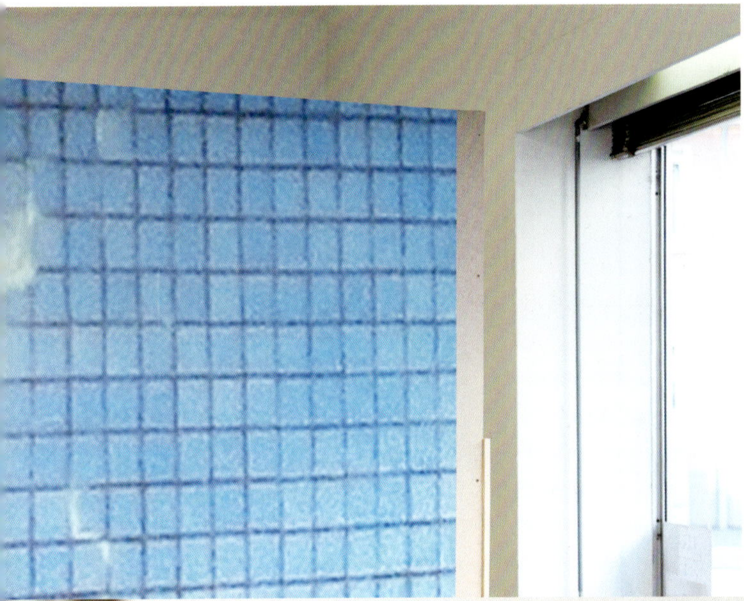

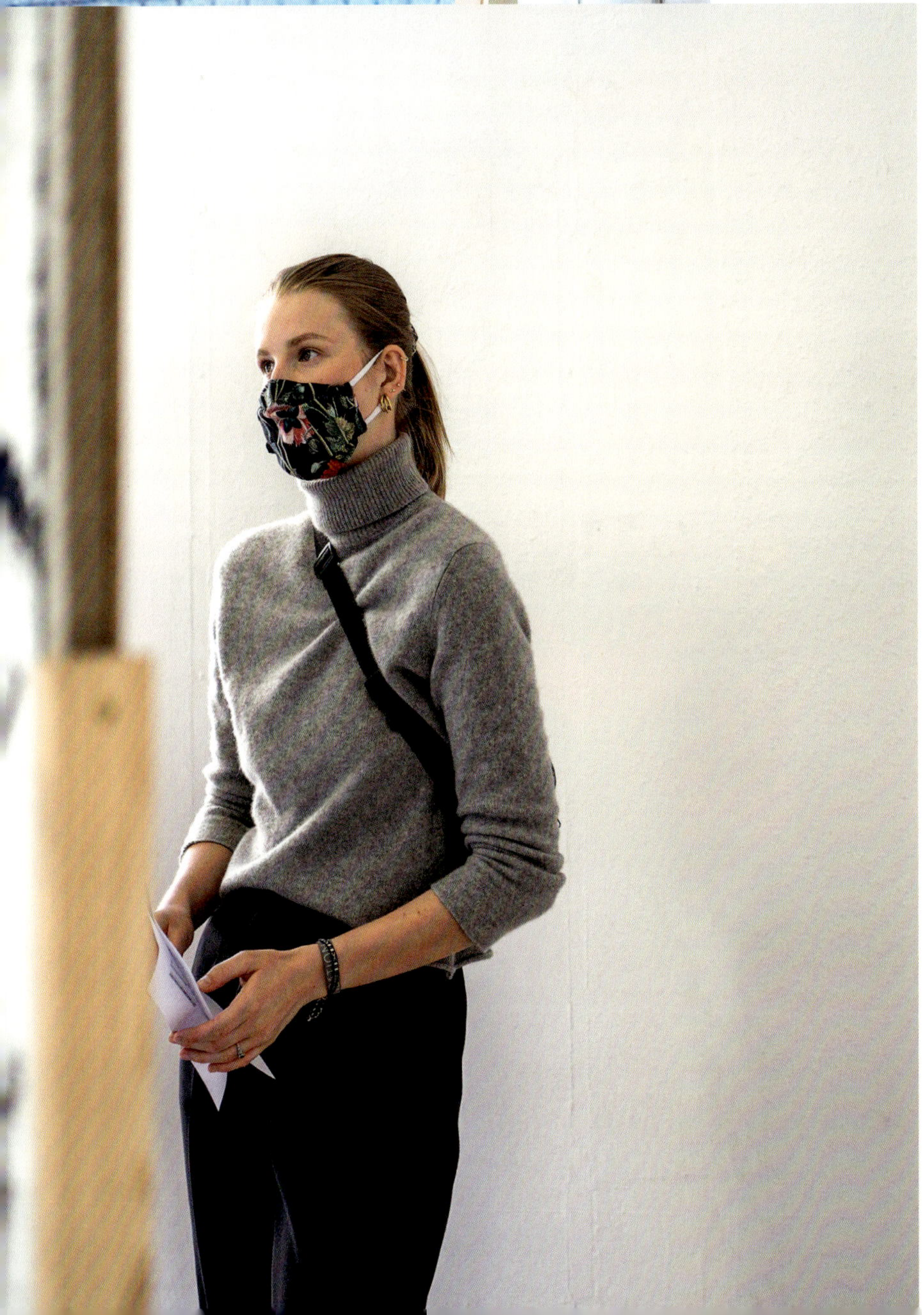

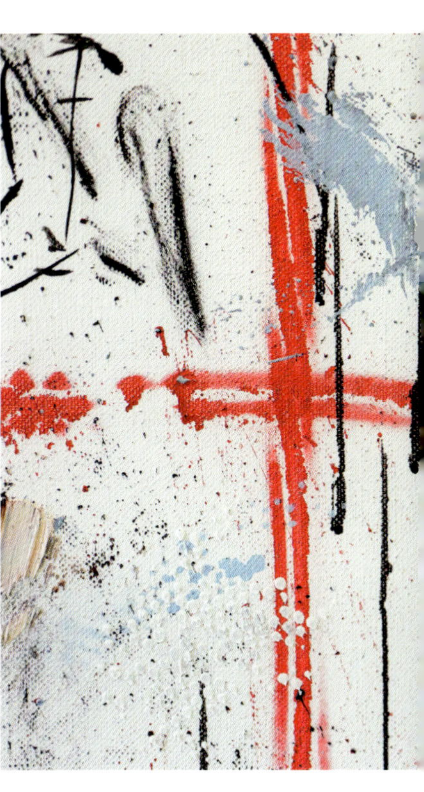

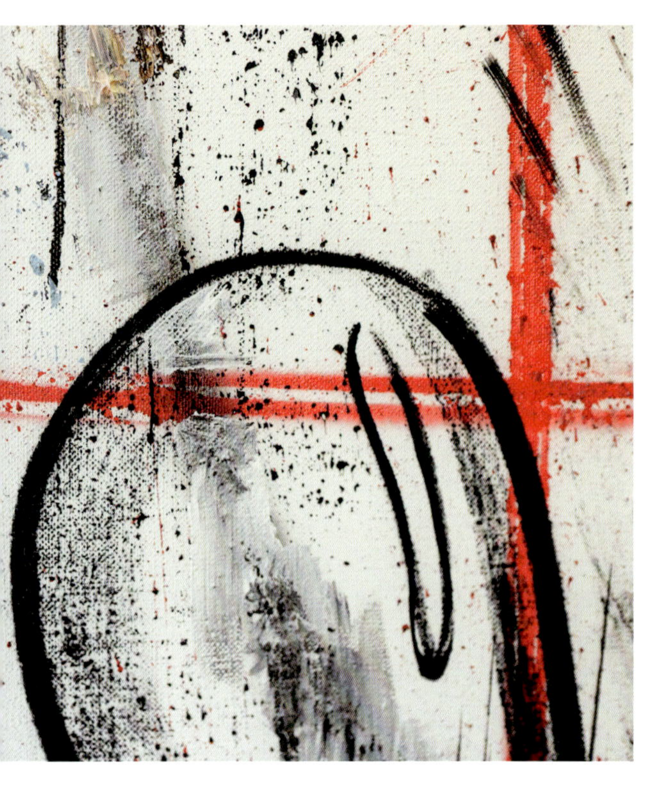

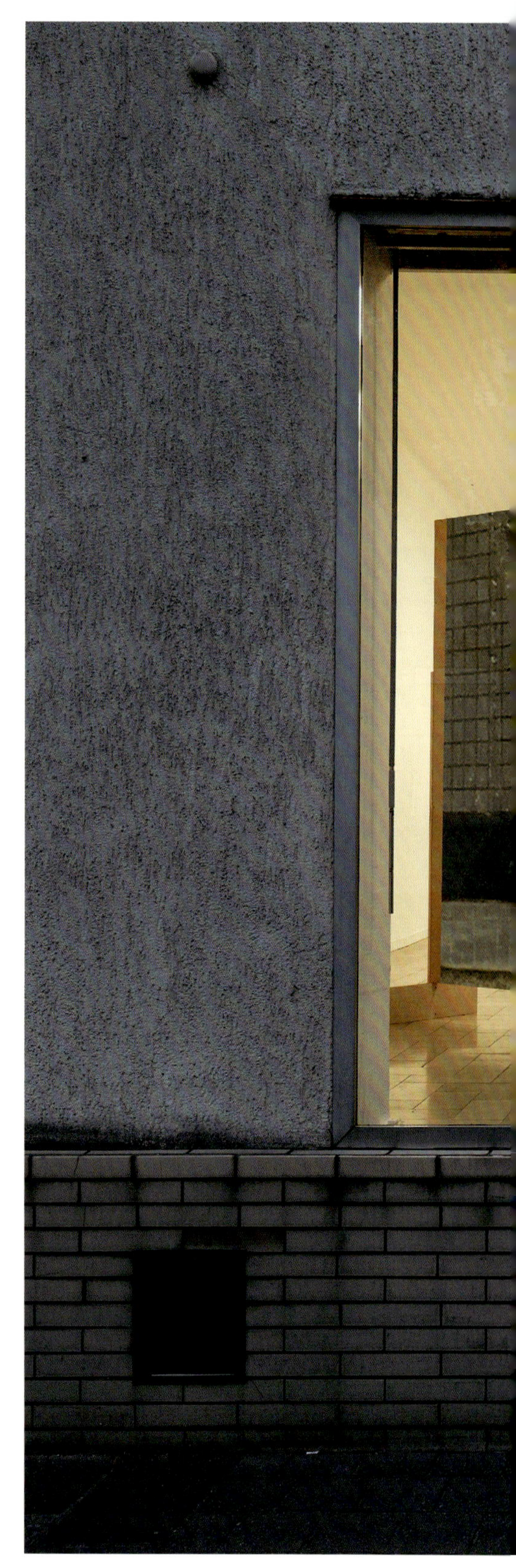

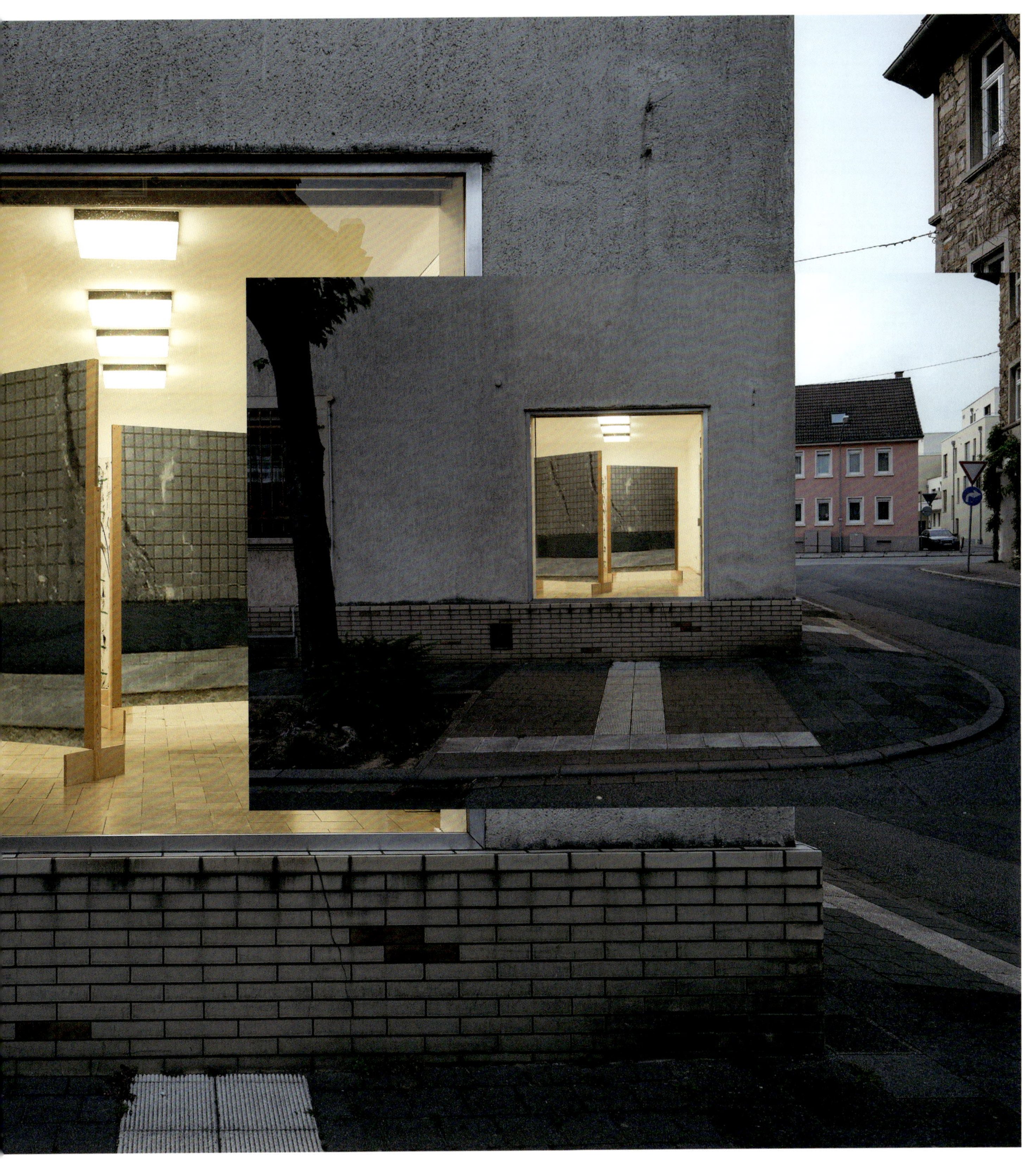

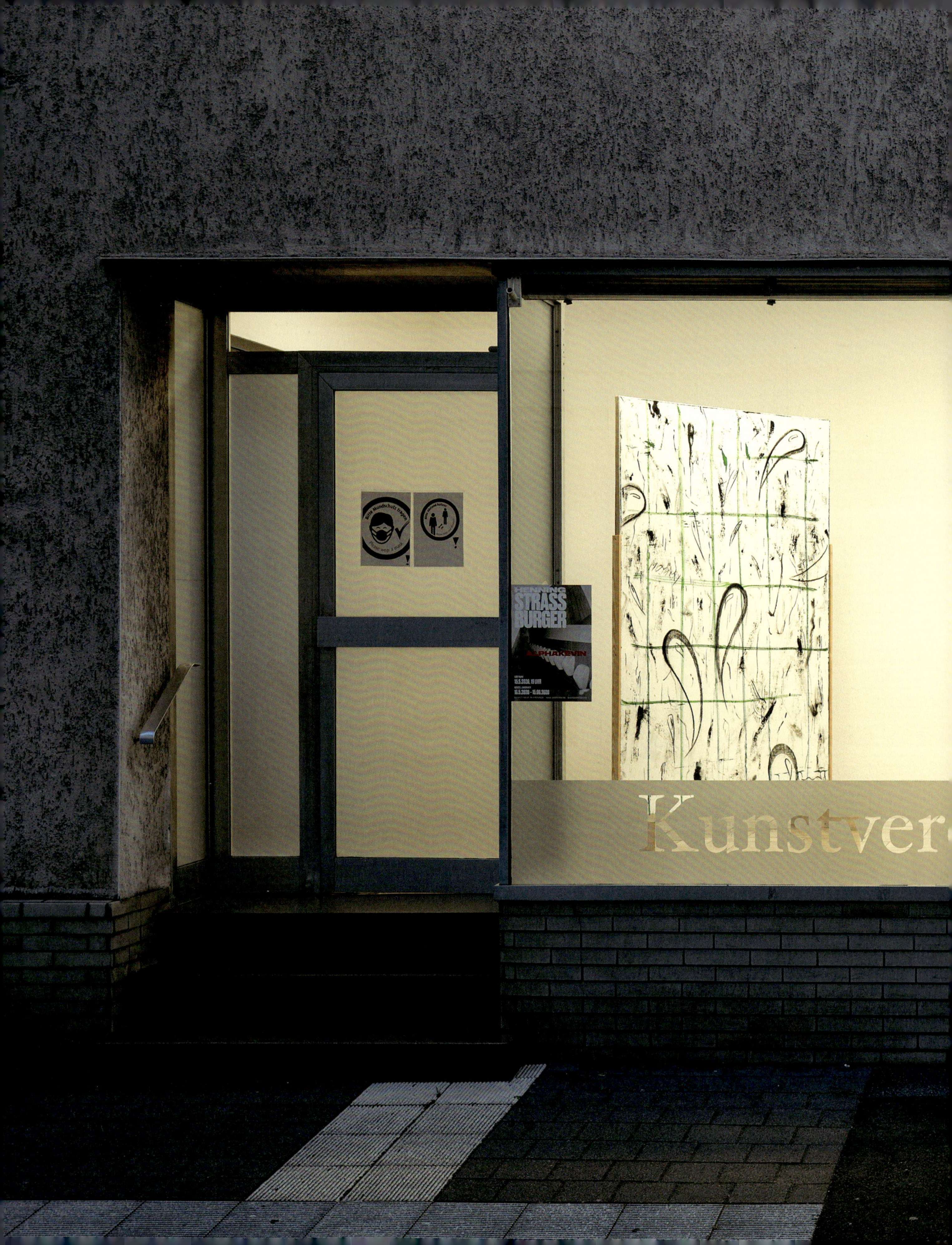

HENNING
STRASS
BURGER
ALPHAKEVIN
15.5.2020, 19 UHR
15.5.2020 – 15.06.2020
Kunstver

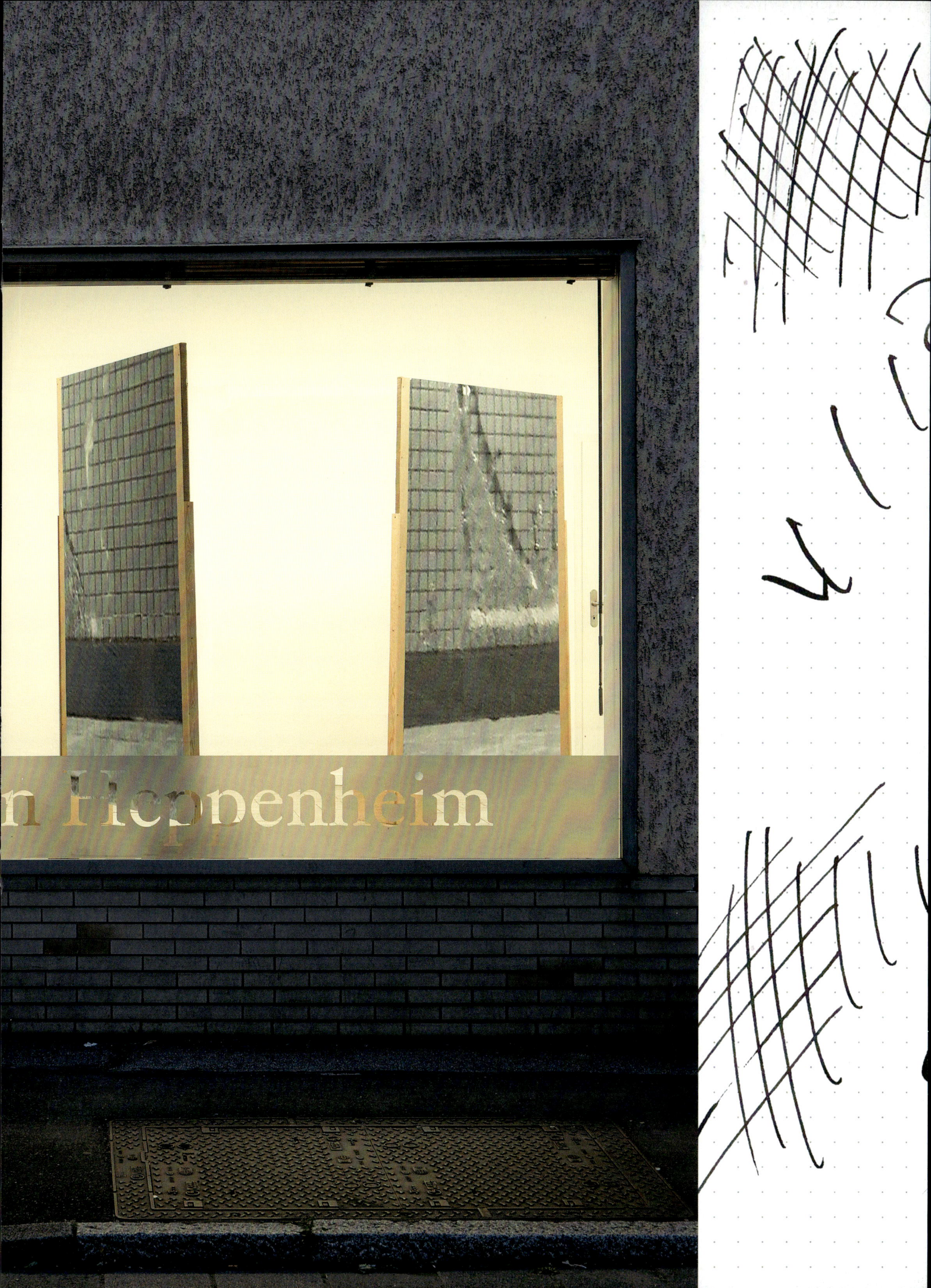
n Heppenheim

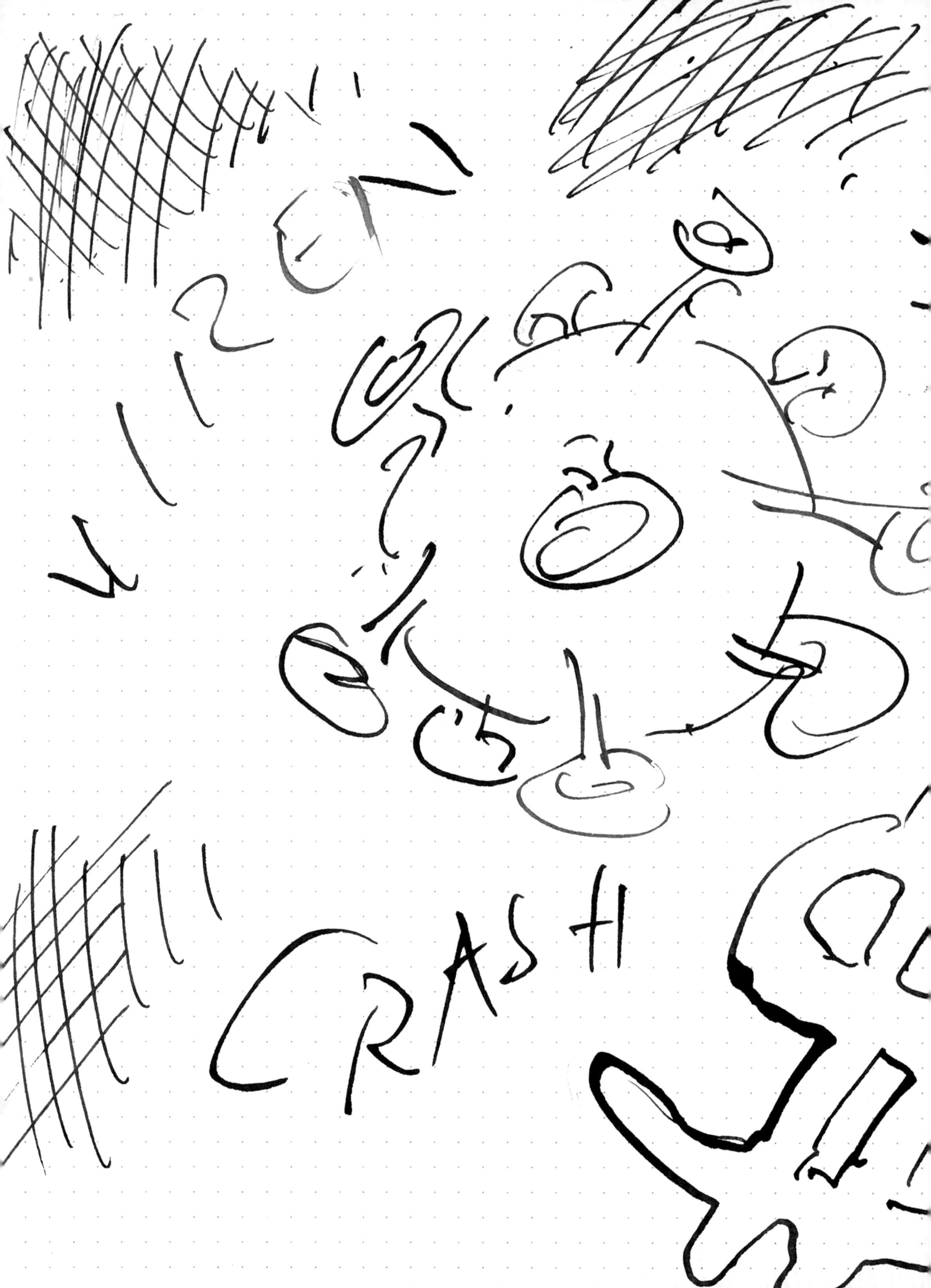

CRASH

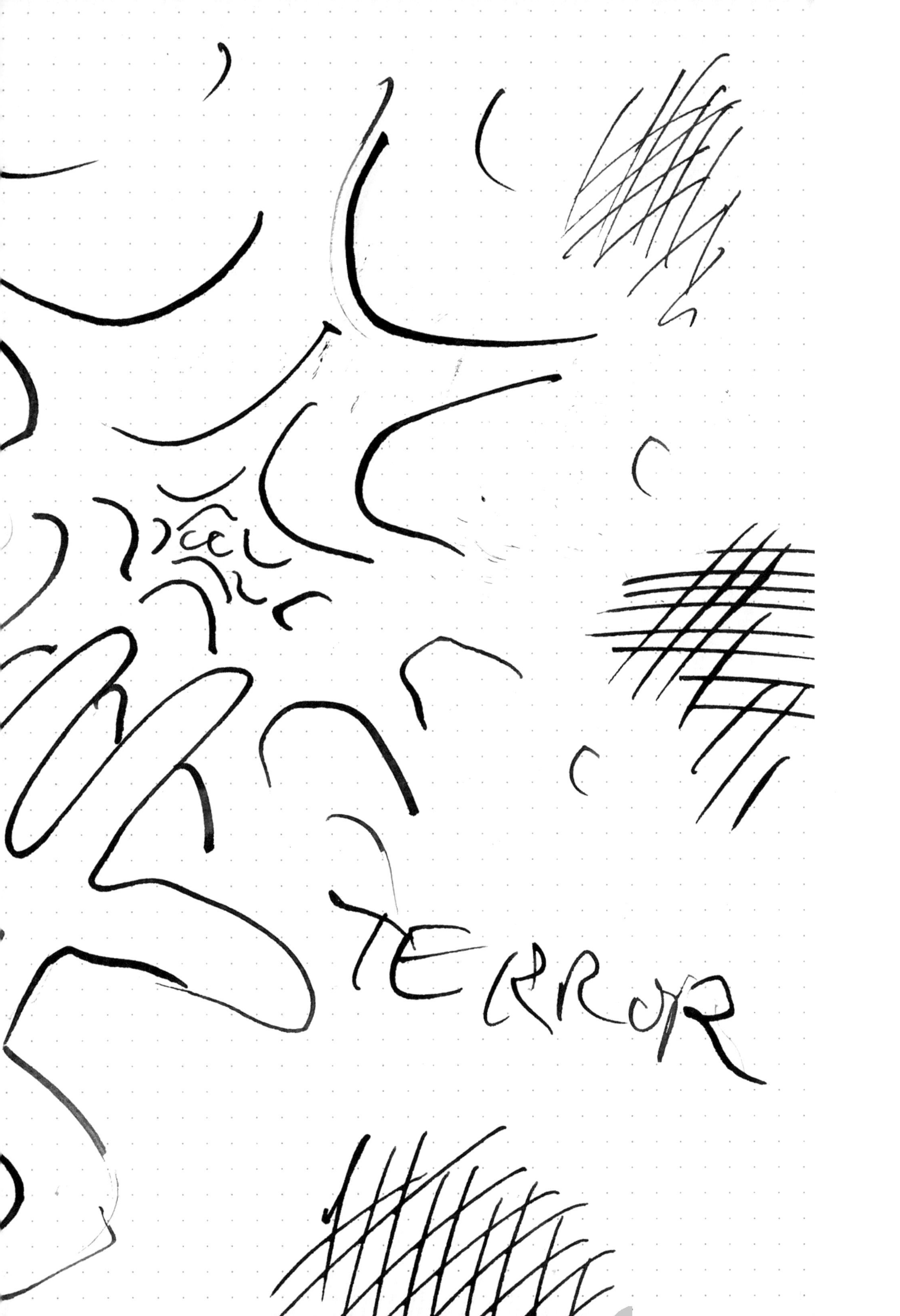

TERROR

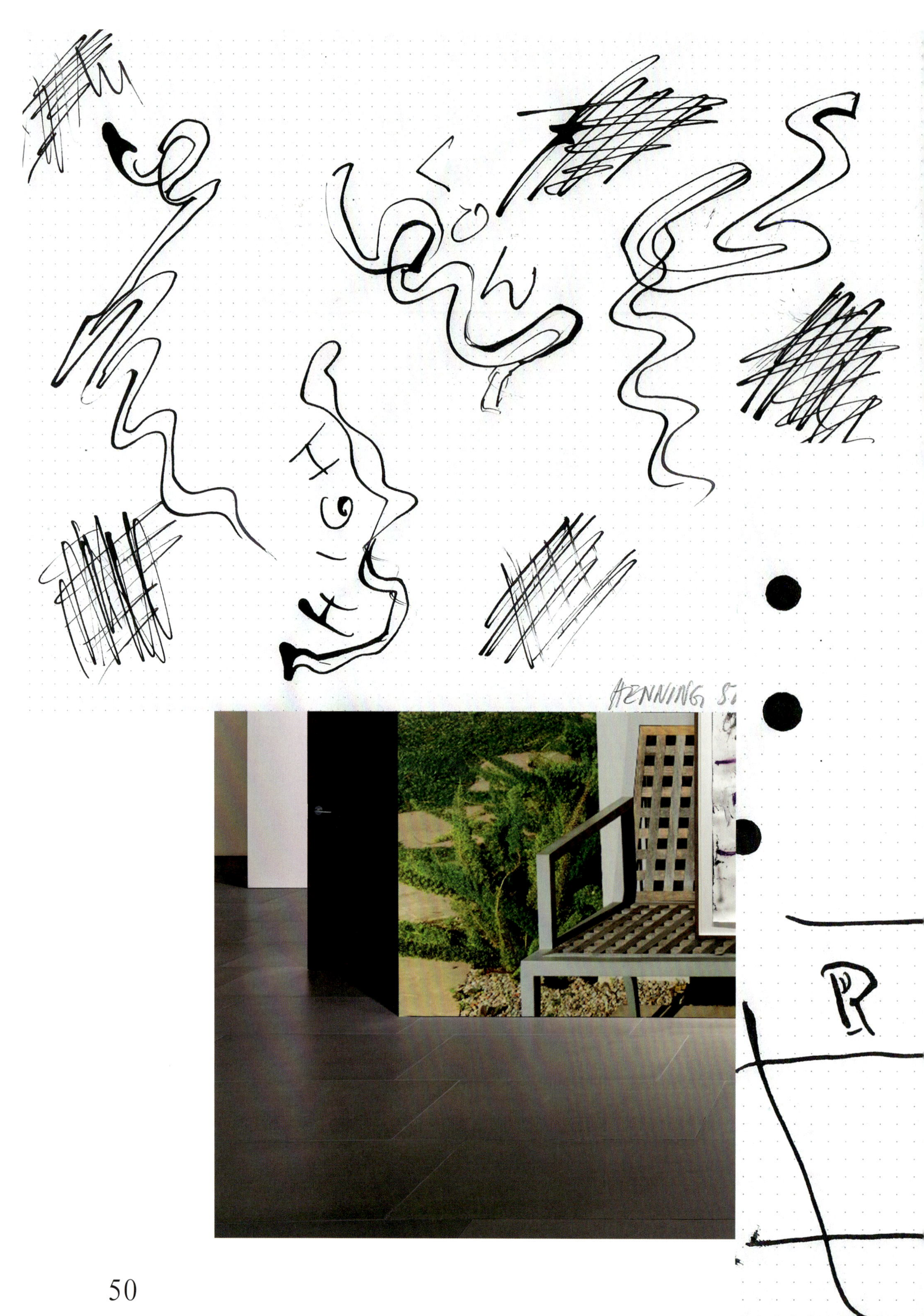

50

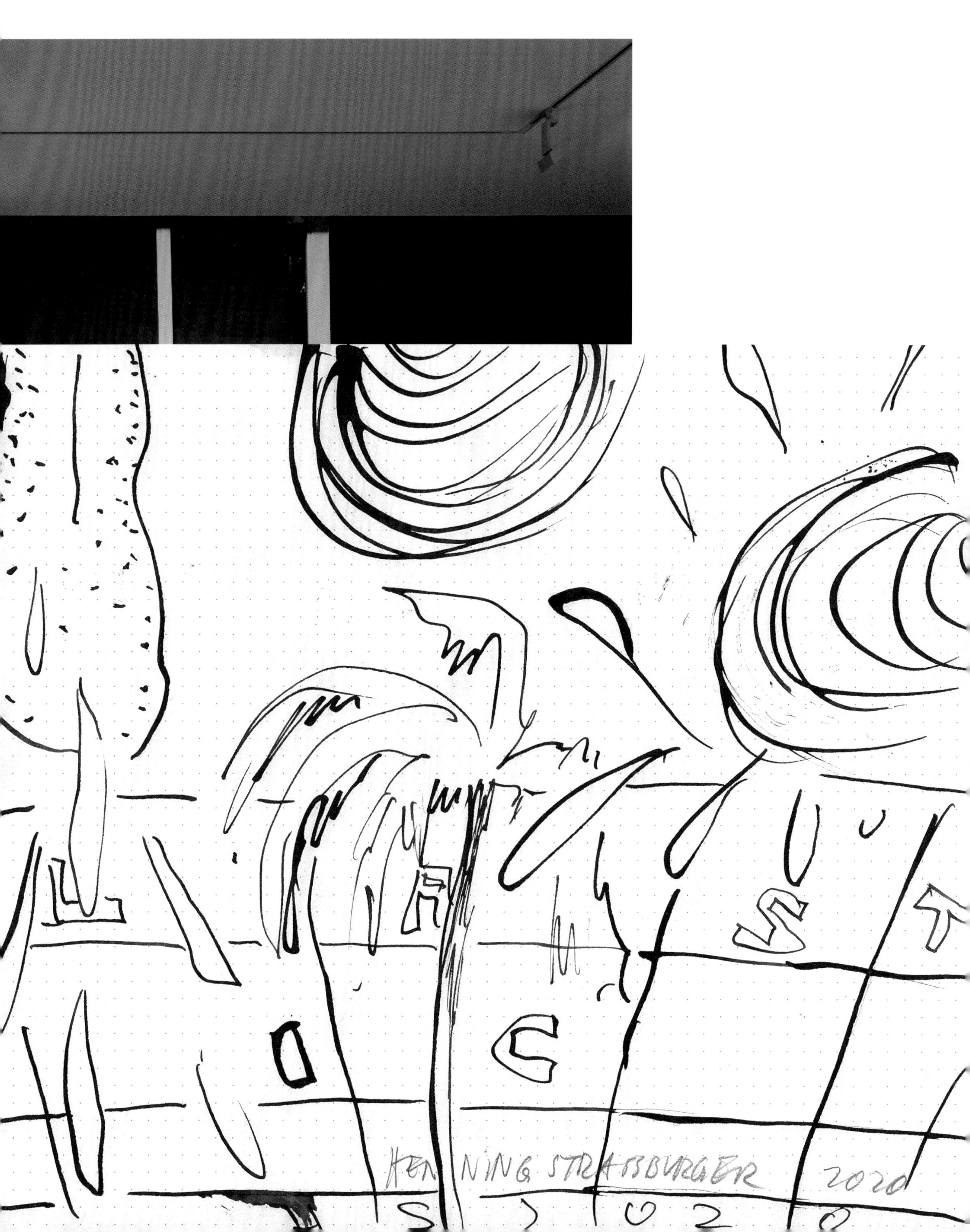

HENNING STRASSBURGER 2020

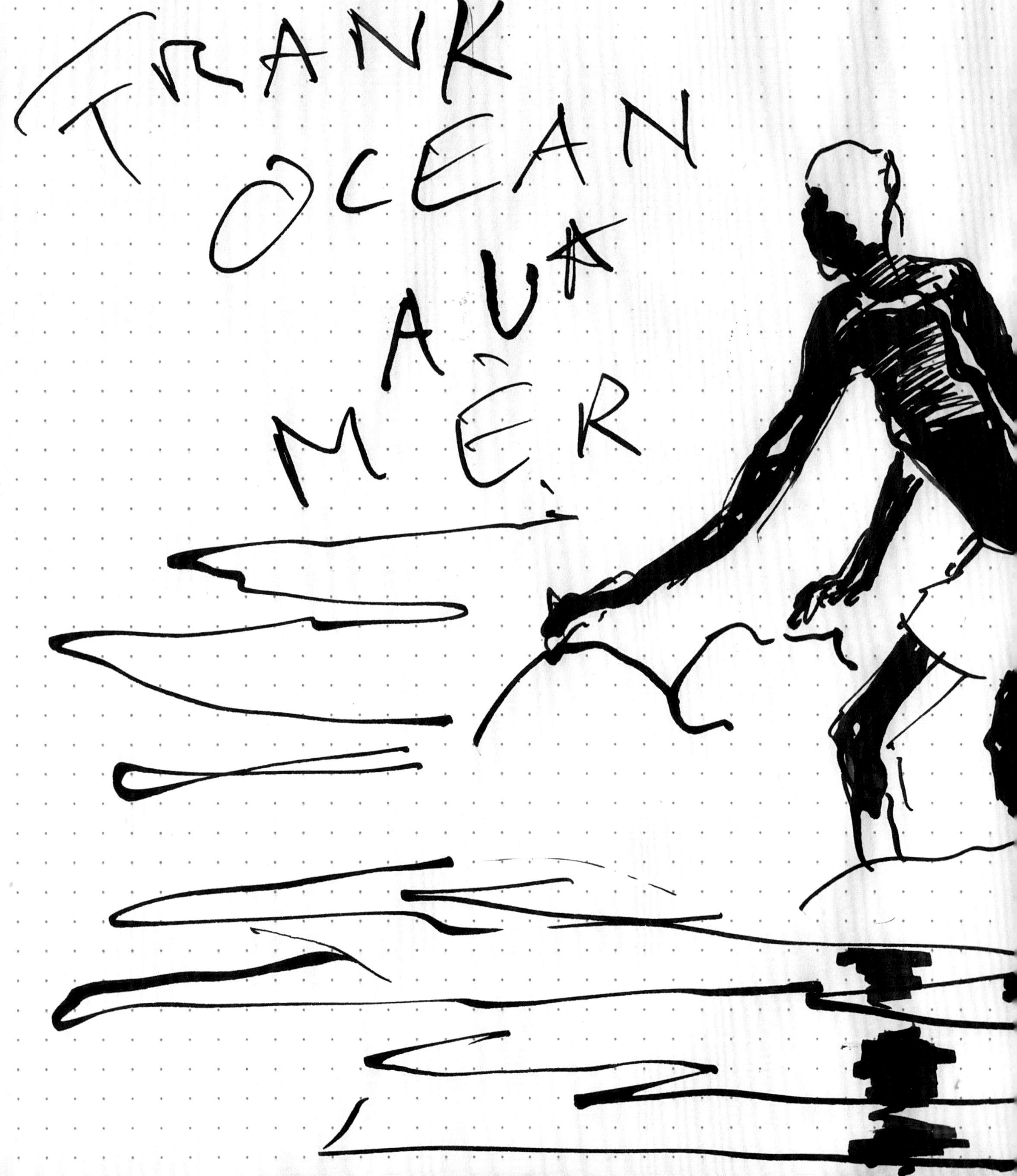
FRANK
OCEAN
AU
MER

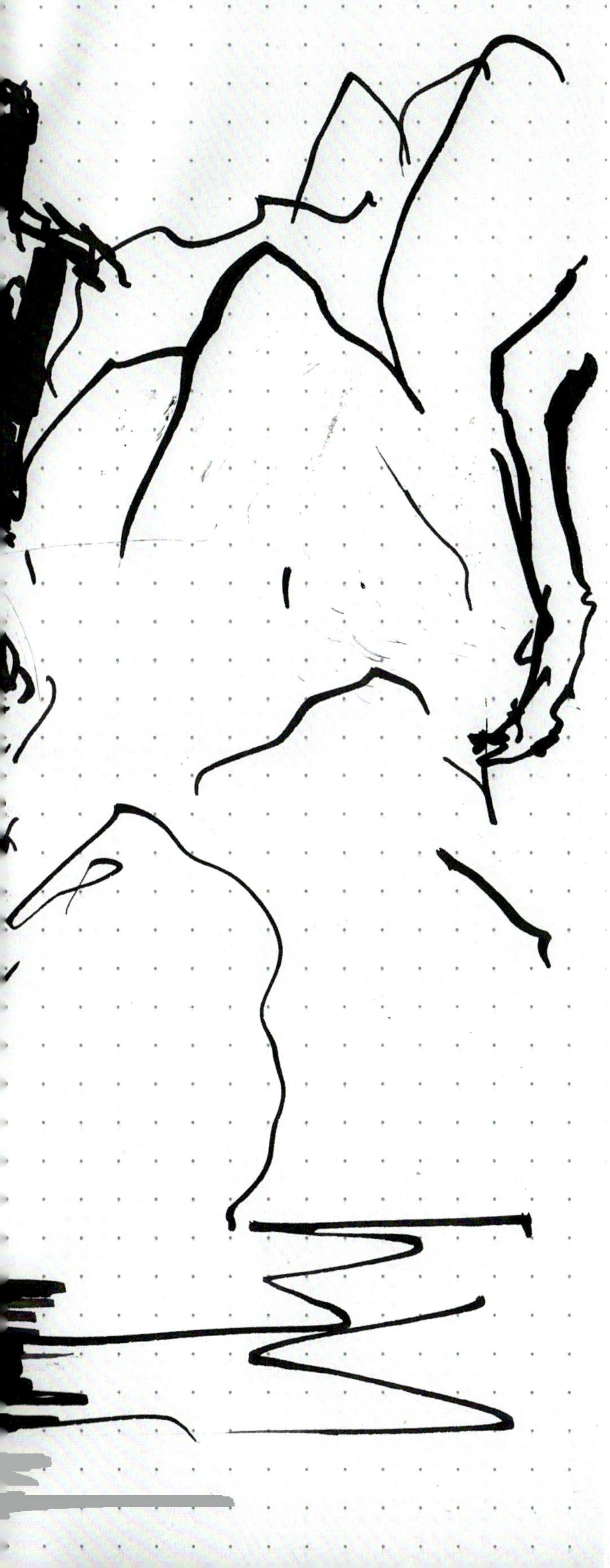

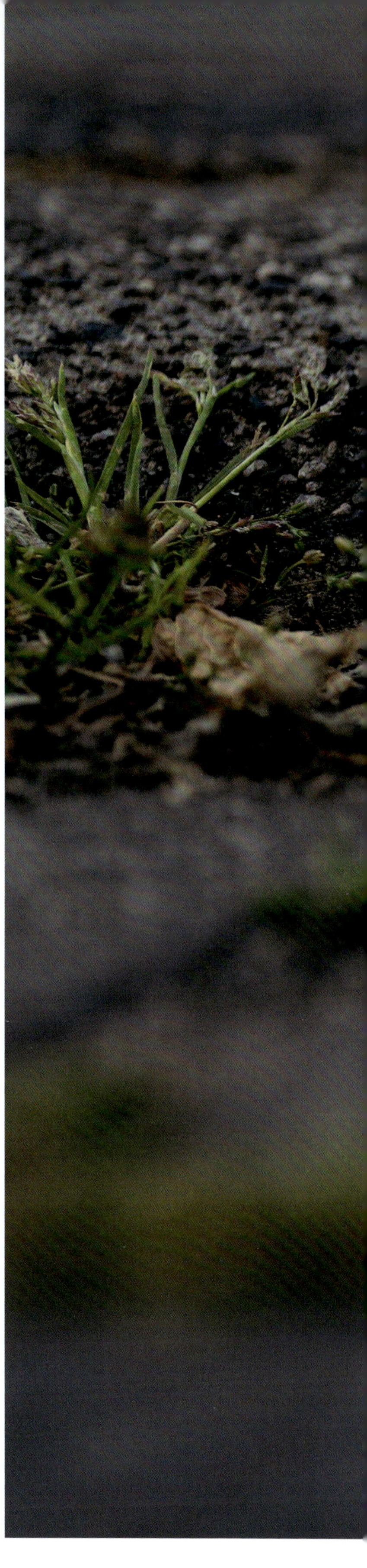

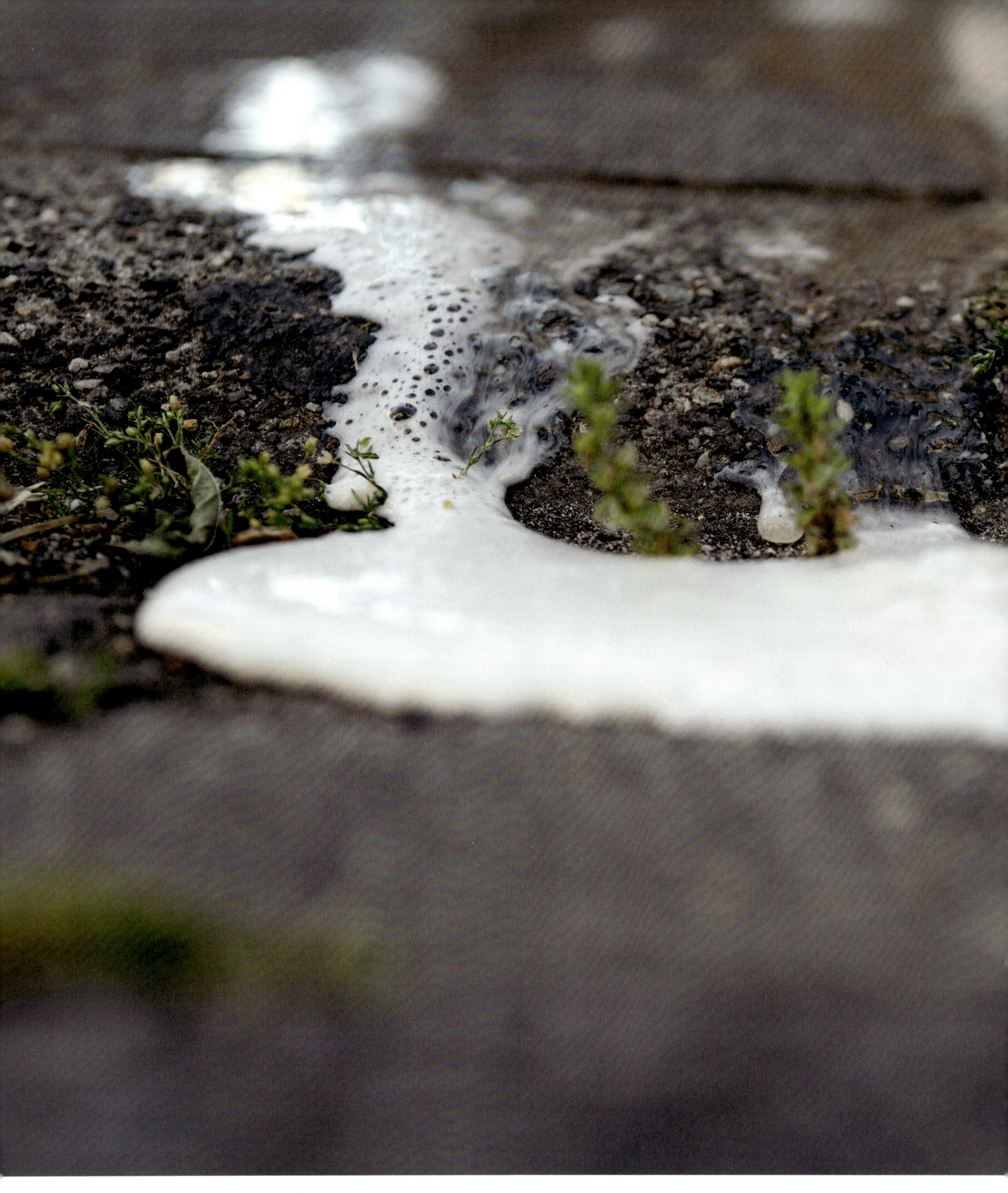

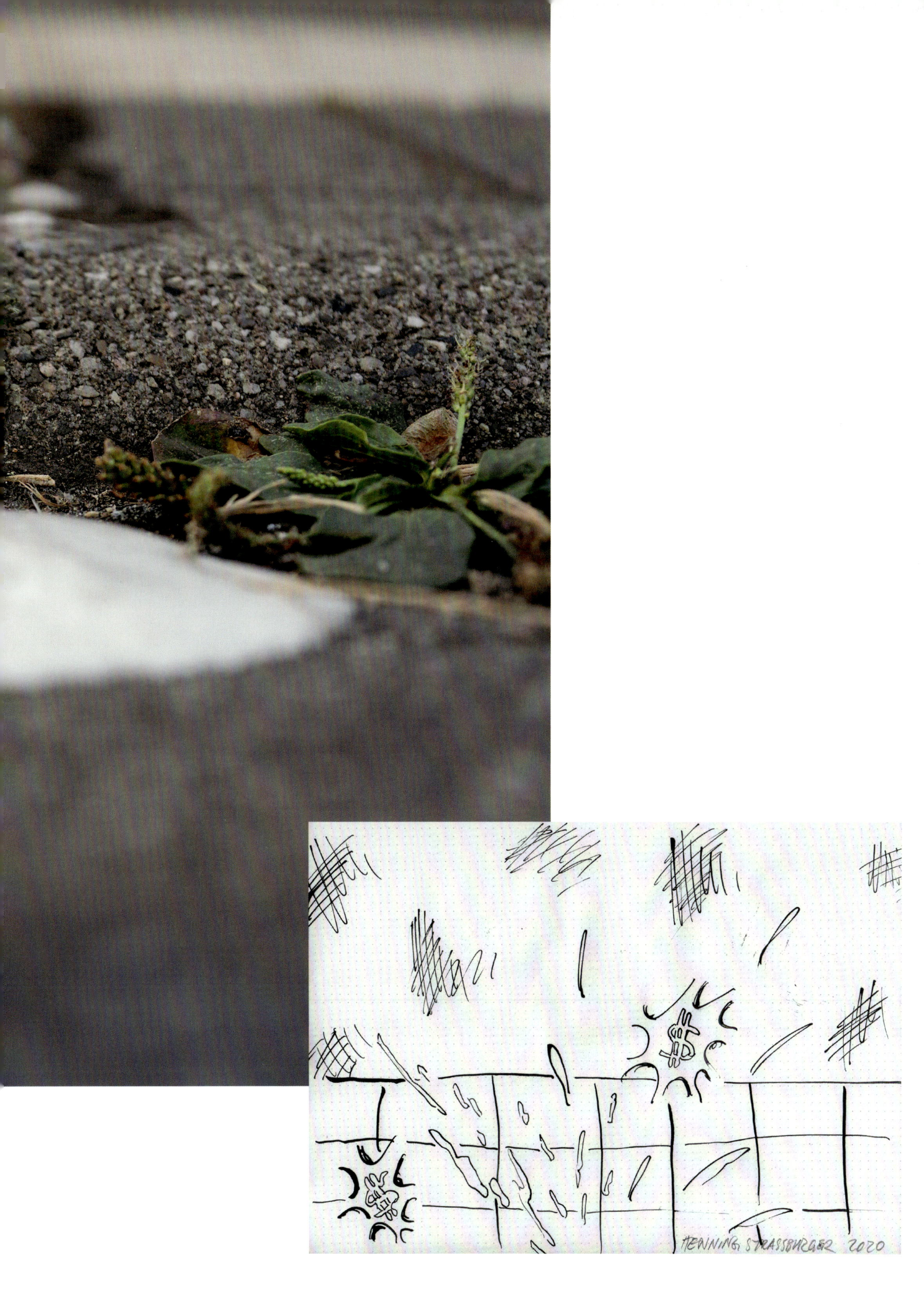

HENNING STRASSBURGER 2020

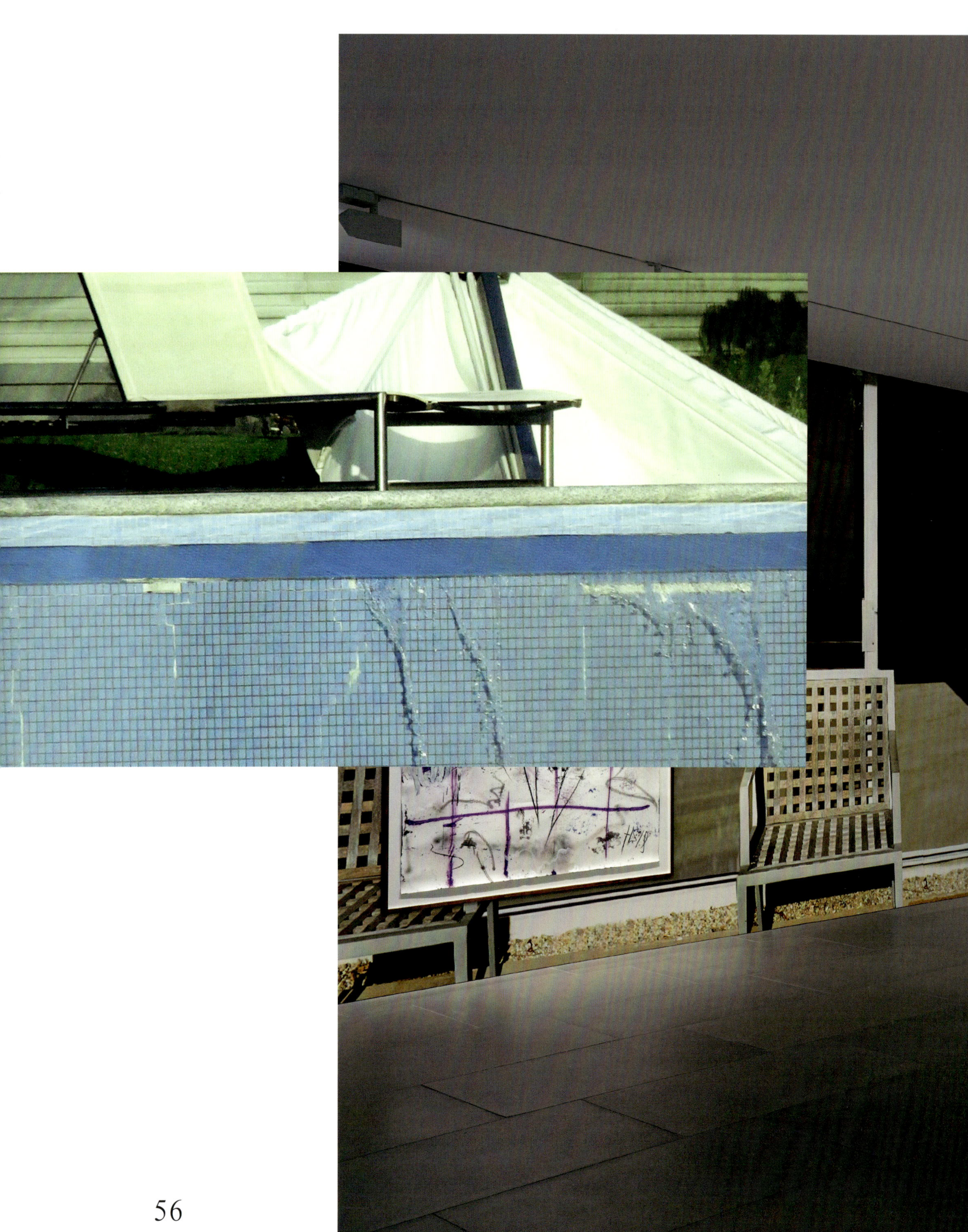

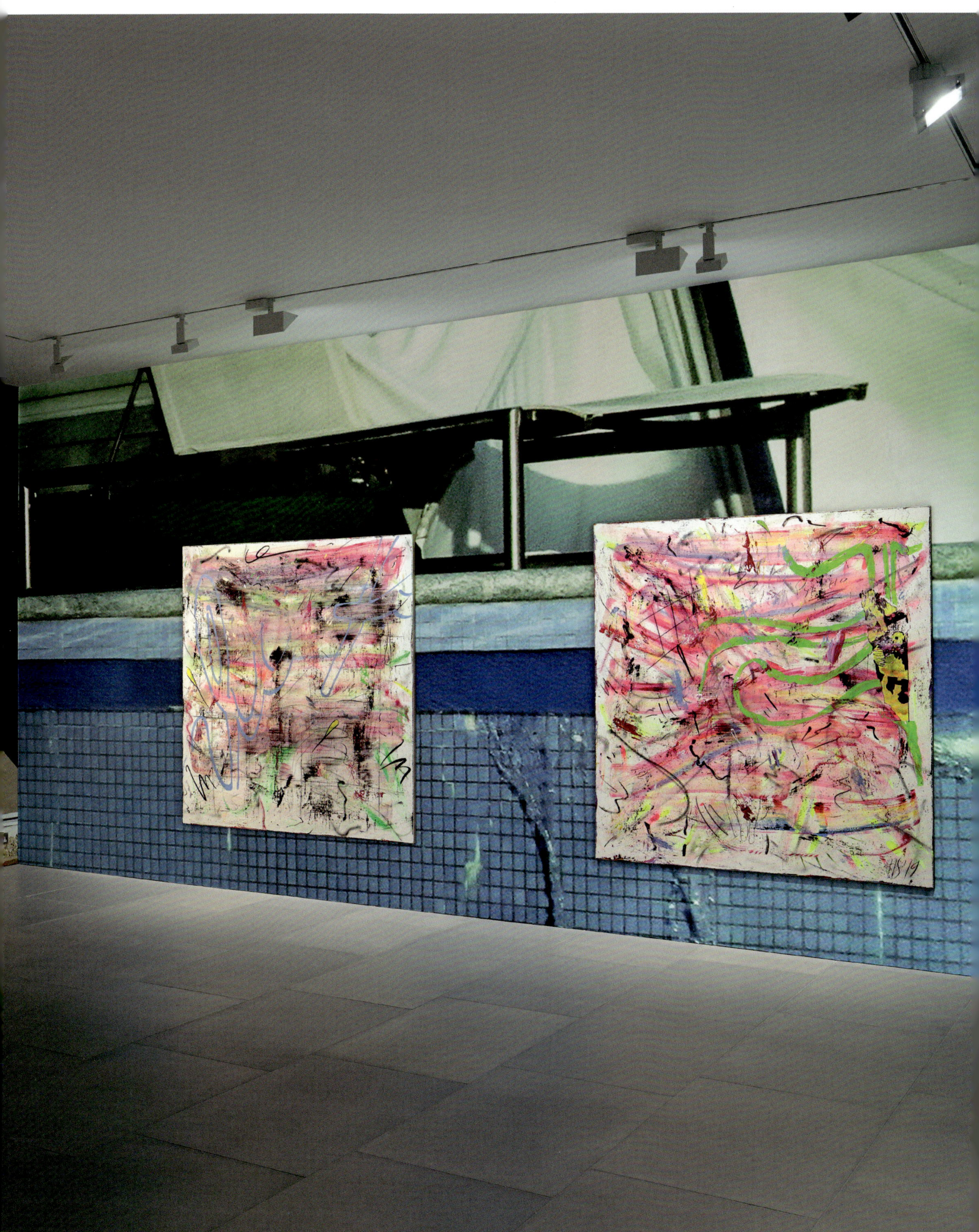

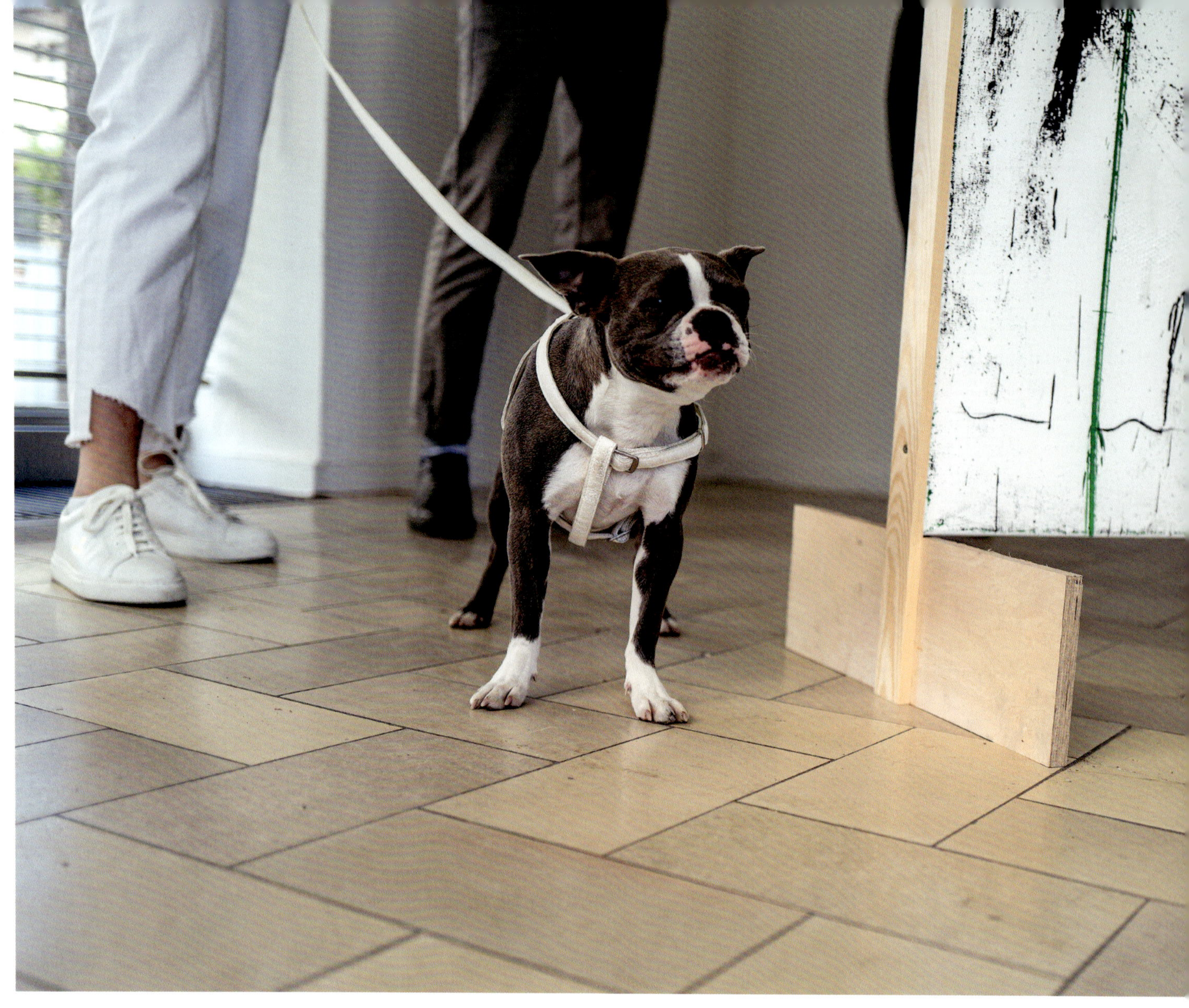

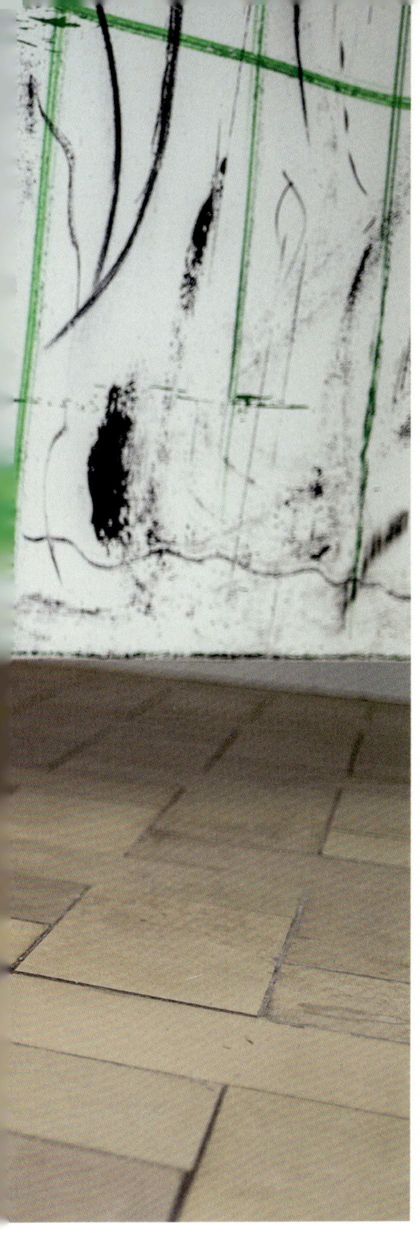

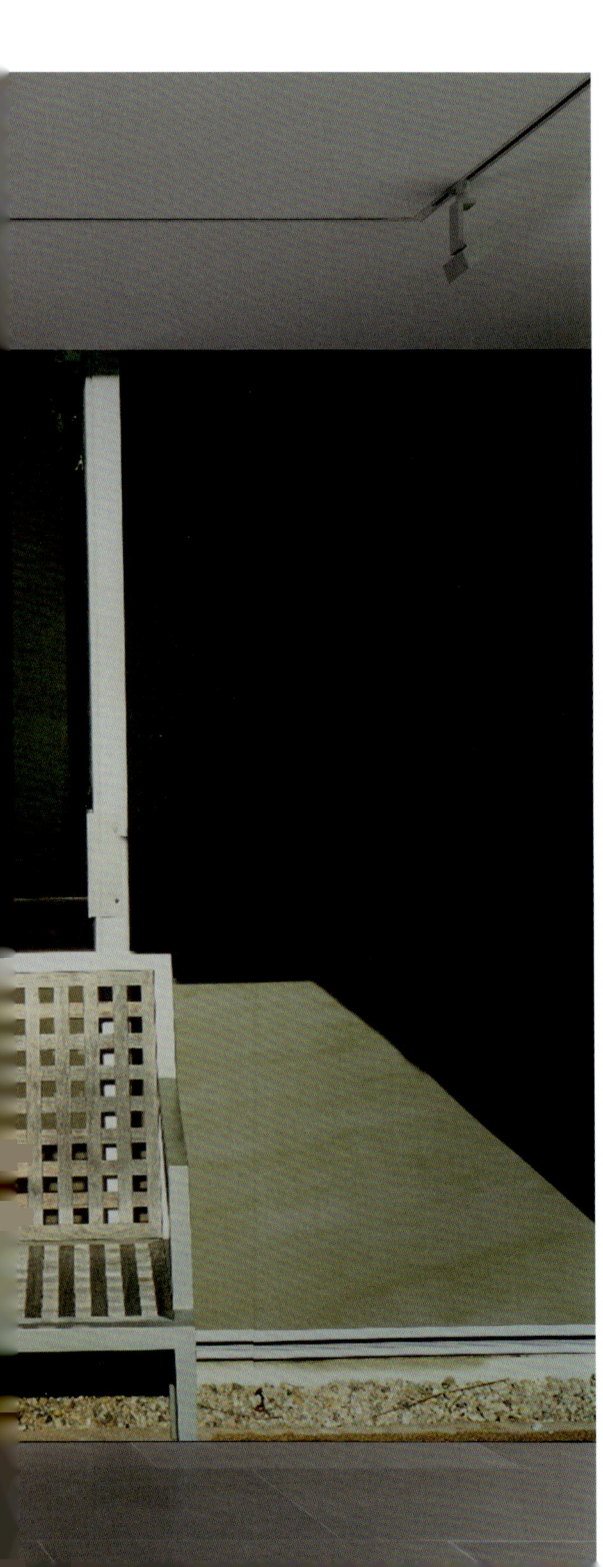

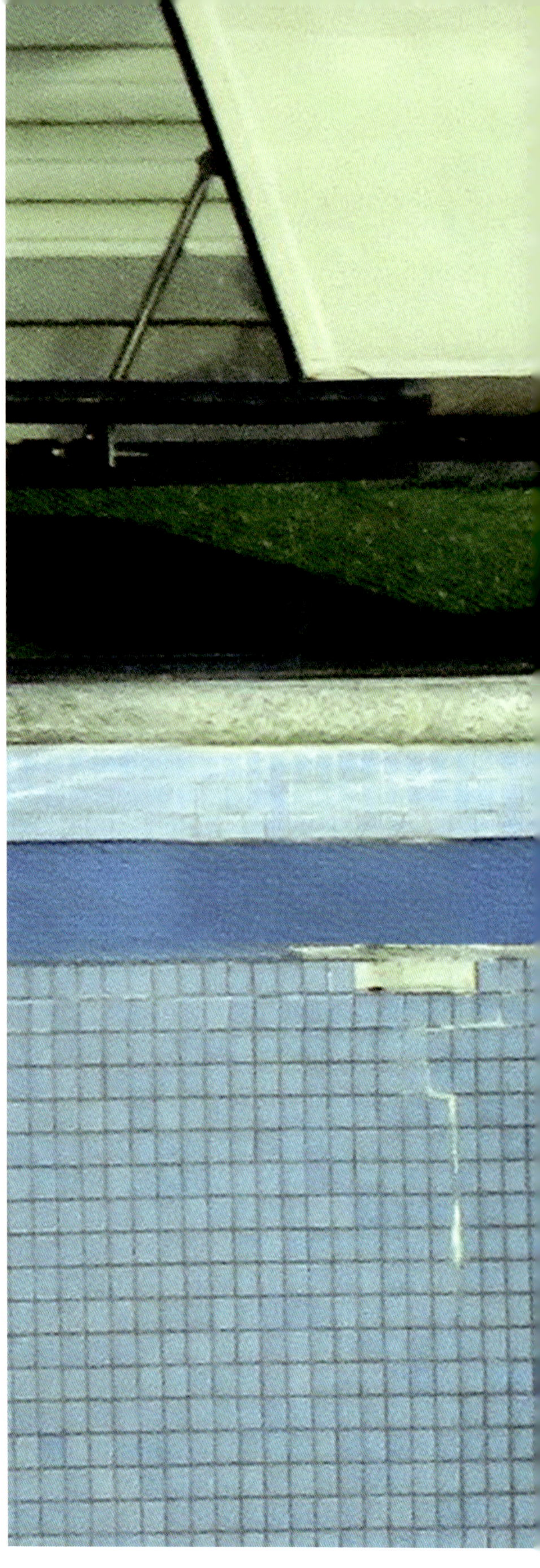

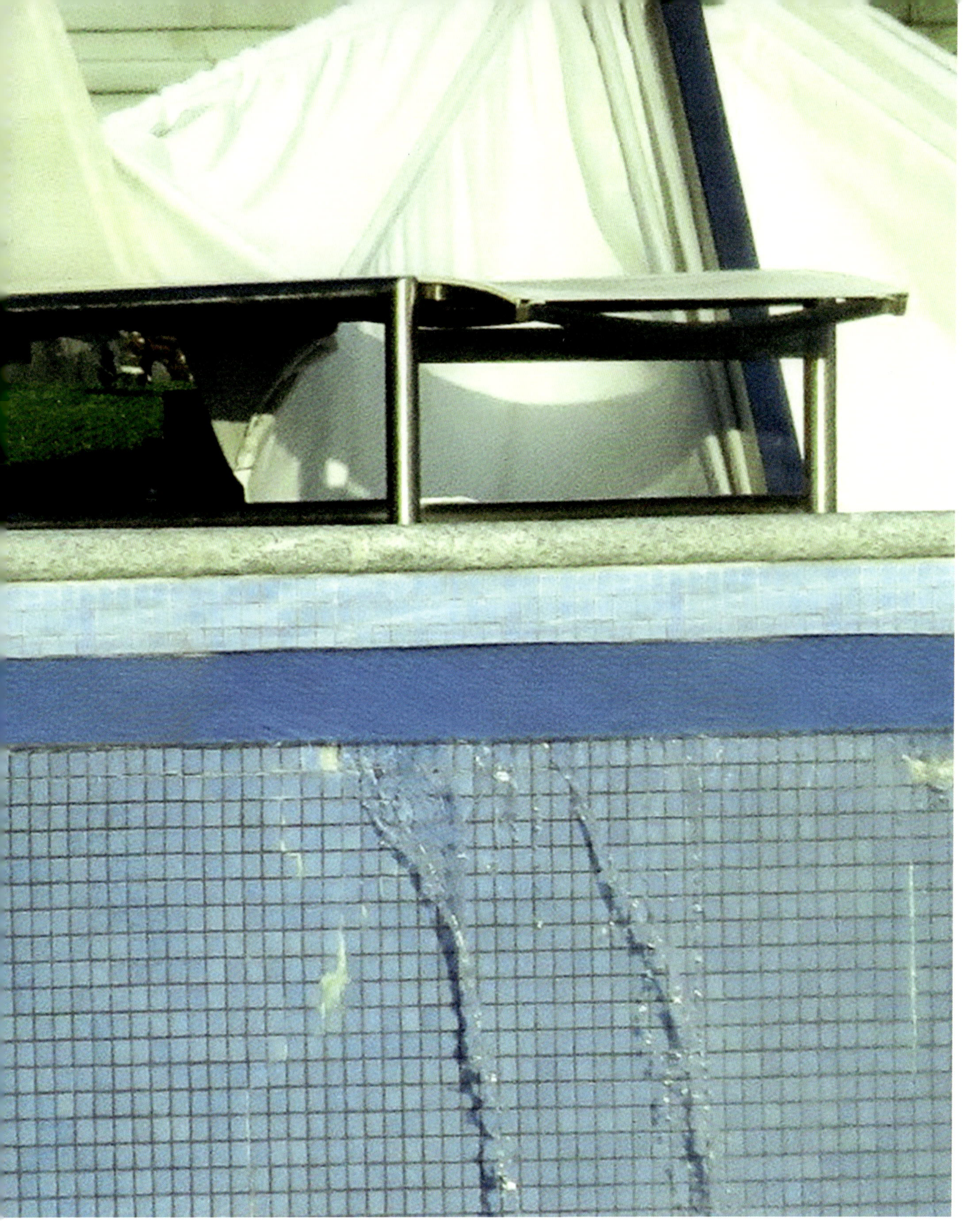

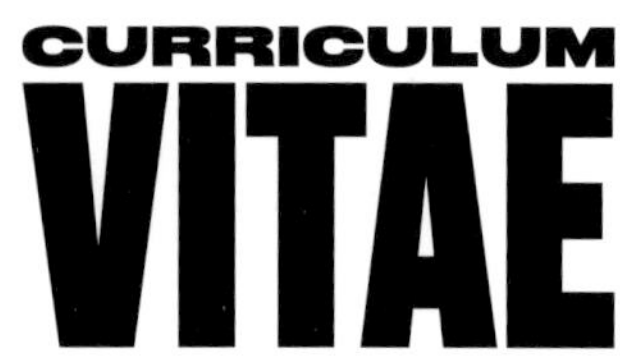

CURRICULUM VITAE

**Henning
Strassburger**

1983
geboren / born in Meißen

2014
Gastprofessur / Visiting Professorship,
University of Nevada, Las Vegas

2015–2016
Vertretungsprofessur / Visiting Professorship, Staatliche Kunstakademie Karlsruhe

lebt und arbeitet / lives and works in Berlin
und Barjols, Frankreich

**Ausgewählte Einzelausstellungen
Selected Solo Exhibitions
* Katalog / Catalogue**

2021
Sies + Höke, Düsseldorf
The Breeder, Athens

2020
Die Unschuldigen,
Contemporary Fine Arts, Berlin*

Alphakevin, Kunstverein Heppenheim*

2019
Karma Mansion, Blain|Southern, London

2018
Kenny, Blain|Southern, Berlin

Air Conditioner, Osnova Gallery,
Moskau / Moscow

Fünf Bilder, Blumenthal, New York

2017
Privacy, Hofstra University Gallery,
New York

Jane, Sies + Höke, Düsseldorf

Private Resort, Múrias | Centeno, Porto

Meditations in an Emergency [MIAE],
Neue Galerie Gladbeck*

2016
Superet Exit Systems, Studiolo,
Mailand / Milan

Bleaching is Teaching, Kunstverein
Reutlingen*

Superet Light, Soy Capitán, Berlin

2015
Dirt Club, BolteLang, Zürich / Zurich

Think Tank, Oldenburger Kunstverein,
Oldenburg*

Pool, Sies + Höke, Düsseldorf

2014
What this does, Salon Dahlmann, Berlin*

Strike the Pose, Soy Capitán, Berlin

2012
indexternal, Soy Capitán, Berlin

I am a Girl, Kavi Gupta Gallery, Chicago

So Athletic, Kunstverein Rosa-Luxemburg-Platz, Berlin (mit / with Wendy White)*

2011
Image, fiebach minninger, Köln / Cologne*

SoftiDrink, Kunstverein Heppenheim*

2010
Good Old Figuration, Kunstsammlung der Deutschen Bundesbank, Frankfurt am Main*

2009
A Kansas City Shuffle, Verein für Raum und Form in der bildenden Kunst, Wien / Vienna

Die Neue Härte, Golden Pudel Club, Hamburg

**Ausgewählte Gruppenausstellungen
Selected Group Exhibitions
* Katalog / Catalogue**

2020
Black Album / White Cube: A Journey into Art and Music, Kunsthal Rotterdam*

Echo Chambers, Galerie Bärbel Grässlin, Frankfurt*

Abstrakte Kunst, Miettinen Collection, Berlin

Kir Royal, Galerie Christine Mayer, München (*Various Others* mit / with Thomas v. Poschinger)

Hallucinogenic, Gerhard Hofland, Amsterdam

A Table for 50, PCP Gallery, Paris

Paranoia Strikes Deep, Osnova Mosco

2019
PIN, Pinakothek der Moderne, München / Munich

Hyper! A Journey into Art and Music, Deichtorhallen, Hamburg*

Image Vision, Philipp Pflug Contemporary, Frankfurt am Main

Painting Zeitgeist?, AchenbachHagemeier, Berlin

You are here: Works from the Peters-Messer Collection, Werkschauhalle Leipzig

A chair, projected, BolteLang, Zürich / Zurich

2018
Trance, Aïshti Foundation, Beirut*

Works on Paper, Gussglashalle, Berlin

Doodle & Disegno, Blain|Southern, Berlin

Paradise is Now: Palm Trees in Art, Robert Grunenberg, Berlin & Salon Dahlmann, Berlin*

2017
Wohnfront Megapark, Plan5, Stockholm

Experimental Berlin, Richard Taittinger Gallery, New York

Quality of Cuties, just married, Osaka

Die linke und die rechte Hand für ein Halleluja, David Achenbach Projects, Wuppertal

Monet is my Church, Dittrich & Schlechtriem, Berlin*

2016
My Abstract World – Works from the Olbricht Collection, me Collectors Room, Berlin

Now Now, nownow.contemporary, Mailand / Milan

I am a golden God, fiebach minninger, Köln / Cologne

Face to Face: The Ernesto Esposito Collection, Palazzo Fruscione, Salerno*

Bundeskunsthalle, Bonn*

2015
Studiolo, Mailand / Milan

2014
New Associations, Salts, Birsfelden

Hausreste, Haus der Kunst, Solothurn

Wo ist hier? #1: Malerei und Gegenwart, Kunstverein Reutlingen

BolteLang, Zürich / Zurich

Luggage and observations, Galerie Klaus Gerrit Friese, Stuttgart*

Unfinished Season, Galerie Nagel+Draxler, Köln / Cologne

2013
The Revenge of the double X Factor (mit / with Hans-Jörg Mayer), Provinz Edition, Essen*

Come, all ye faithful, Florian Christopher, Zürich / Zurich

The Digital Divide, Sies + Höke, Düsseldorf

ReMap 4: In the Studio, Kunsthalle Athena, Athen / Athens

Berlin.Status (2), Künstlerhaus Bethanien, Berlin*

Freie Sicht, Nassauischer Kunstverein, Wiesbaden*

Provinz Editionen, Galerie Vera Gliem, Köln / Cologne

Hotel International, Chelsea Hotel, Köln / Cologne

Get off the Lawn, Parade Ground, New York

Deep Cuts, Anna Kustera Gallery, New York

2012
Bilderladen DuMont-Carré, Galerie Christian Nagel, Köln / Cologne & fiebach minninger, Köln / Cologne

Paradise City, Autocenter, Berlin

Infernoesque (mit / with Adrian Buschmann), Berlin

2011
Abstract Ilona, Kavi Gupta Gallery, Berlin*

Index11, Kunsthaus Hamburg*

MDFA – Sammlung im Alpenhof, Oberegg

Vandel 7. Sozialgestaltung: Liebe + Friedhof, Hospitalhof, Stuttgart*

2010
Informal Relations, Museum of Contemporary Art, Indianapolis*

IMPRESSUM
COLOPHON

Diese Publikation erscheint anlässlich der Ausstellung / this publication is published to accompany the exhibition:

**HENNING STRASSBURGER
ALPHAKEVIN
16.5. – 15.6.2020**

Kunstverein Heppenheim e.V.
Bahnhofstrasse 1
64646 Heppenheim

Herausgeber / Editor
Dr. Uwe Emig

Redaktion / Editorial staff
Henning Strassburger
Christian Malycha

Gestaltung / Design
Enver Hadzijaj

Übersetzungen / Translations
Alexander Serner

Installationsfotografie
Johannes Kaiser, Heppenheim

**Projektmanagement /
Project management, Kerber Verlag**
Verena Simon

**Herstellung / Production,
Kerber Verlag**
Jens Bartneck

**Gesamtherstellung /
Printed and published by**
Kerber Verlag, Bielefeld
Windelsbleicher Str. 166–170
33659 Bielefeld
Germany
+49 (0) 5 21/9 50 08-10
+49 (0) 5 21/9 50 08-88 (F)
info@kerberverlag.com
kerberverlag.com

Kerber Publikationen werden weltweit vertrieben / Kerber publications are distributed worldwide:

ACC Art Books
Sandy Lane
Old Martlesham
Woodbridge, IP12 4SD
UK
+44 1394 38 99 50
+44 1394 38 99 99 (F)
accartbooks.com

Artbook | D.A.P.
75 Broad Street, Suite 630
New York, NY 10004
USA
+1 212 627 19 99
+1 212 627 94 84 (F)
artbook.com

AVA Verlagsauslieferung AG
Centralweg 16
8910 Affoltern am Albis
Switzerland
+41 44 762 42 50
+41 44 762 42 10 (F)
avainfo@ava.ch

KNV Zeitfracht
Verlagsauslieferung
kerber-verlag@knv-zeitfracht.de

Die Deutsche Nationalbibliothek verzeichnet diese Publikation in der Deutschen Nationalbibliografie: dnb.de. / The Deutsche Nationalbibliothek lists this publication in the Deutsche Nationalbibliografie: dnb.de.

© 2021 Kerber Verlag, Bielefeld / Berlin, Henning Strassburger, Andreas Breunig

Alle Rechte vorbehalten. Kein Teil dieses Werkes darf in irgendeiner Form ohne schriftliche Genehmigung des Verlages reproduziert oder unter Verwendung elektronischer Systeme verarbeitet, vervielfältigt oder verbreitet werden. / All rights reserved. No part of this publication may be reproduced, translated, stored in a retrieval system or transmitted in any form or by any means, electronic, mechanical, photocopying or recording or otherwise, without the prior permission of the publisher.

ISBN 978-3-7356-0715-7

www.kerberverlag.com

Printed in Germany